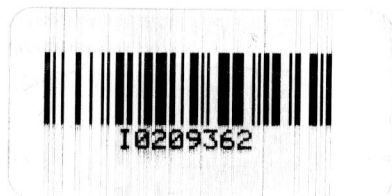

Anonymous

The Sesqui-Centennial

The 150th Anniversary Of The Deerfield Presbyterian Church

Anonymous

The Sesqui-Centennial
The 150th Anniversary Of The Deerfield Presbyterian Church

ISBN/EAN: 9783337113339

Printed in Europe, USA, Canada, Australia, Japan

Cover: Foto ©Lupo / pixelio.de

More available books at **www.hansebooks.com**

1737 — 1887

THE SESQUI-CENTENNIAL,

—OR,—

THE 150th ANNIVERSARY

—OF THE—

DEERFIELD PRESBYTERIAN CHURCH,

CUMBERLAND COUNTY, NEW JERSEY.

CELEBRATED THURSDAY, AUG. 25TH, 1887.

HISTORICAL SERMON, ADDRESSES, &C.

BRIDGETON, N. J.:
JOHN CHEESMAN, PRINTER, PATRIOT OFFICE,
1888.

AN INTRODUCTION.

One of the greatest events known in the history of Deerfield, N. J., was the 150th Anniversary of the Presbyterian Church, held August 25th, 1887. It is estimated that from 1000 to 1200 persons were present. From 700 to 800 people took dinner and supper at the chapel provided for by the congregation. The church was crowded during the three sessions; and part of the time it was calculated that there were as many persons on the outside of the building as inside. A large awning was stretched along the eastern side of the building, with camp stools underneath to accommodate the multitude on the outside, who were unable to gain access to the inside.

The church was tastefully and beautifully decorated for the occasion. No pains were spared to give it an unusually attractive appearance. The music was excellent and could not be surpassed. The choir was assisted by four additional instruments of music. The services were of the most interesting character. The history of the church had been prepared by the pastor, Rev. A. J. Snyder, and read on that occasion, which occupied about an hour and fifteen minutes. The Rev. R. Hamill Davis, Ph. D., a former pastor, talked on "Recollections." He referred touchingly to many incidents which occurred during his ministry here. The Hon. Clifford Stanley Sims, of Mount Holly, N. J., was present and made a few well chosen remarks. He is the great, great, grand-son of the Rev. John Brainerd, who lies buried beneath this church. The Rev. Allen H. Brown gave a very interesting account of the "The Presbyterian Church in South Jersey, its Origin and Progress." Mr. Caleb Allen, A. B., Principal of the West Jersey Academy, made a very entertaining address on the "Important Events of the past one hundred and fifty years." The Rev. Robert J. Burtt and Mr. Charles S. Tyler, sons of former pastors, offered short, yet appreciative addresses, referring to the church in former days.

The Rev. James D. Hunter, a former pastor, made a very elaborate address on the "Sabbath School, its history and work." Revs. David and William James, brothers, and in early life connected with this church, were present and made short and stirring addresses, relative to their early experiences in this connection. Rev. F. R. Brace addressed the congregation on "The Church, and why we should love it." His remarks were appropriate and impressive. This closed the exercises of the occasion, all of which were exceedingly gratifying and profitable, and very much appreciated by all present. The day was beautiful, and the occasion one that will long be remembered by all in atttendance.   A. J. S.,

Deerfield Parsonage.

EXPLANATORY.

On the day of the Anniversary it was resolved by a popular vote of the congregation to have the history of the church published, the Hon. Clifford Stanley Sims, of Mount Holly, N. J., having offered to contribute $20 towards defraying the expense of the publication. Whereupon the pastor of the church Rev. A. J. Snyder, Rev. Allen H. Brown and Rev. R. Hamill Davis, Ph. D., were appointed a committee to carry the resolution into effect. At the close of the exercises the pastor, one of the committee, appointed a Finance Committee to solicit contributions and secure subscribers in order to justify the Publication Committee in making arrangements to publish the pamphlet.

In due time the Finance Committee made their report, which was so flattering that it was deemed safe to undertake the work of publishing the proceedings of the occasion, with the long addresses condensed. The Finance Committee consisted of Messrs. Robert Moore, Sr., Robert Peacock, John Ott, J. Barron Potter, M. D., of Bridgeton, and Mrs. Edo O. Leake.

In the preparation of the history of the church, the pastor gratefully acknowledges his indebtedness both to friends in the congregation and out of it, for historical matter; thus enabling him to give a fuller statement of facts and make the history more replete with interest. It is now submitted to the public, at their own request, together with the other addresses, with the hope that it will prove acceptable and profitable to the people, and serve as a valuable document for reference, both to this generation and the generations yet to come.

The thanks of the pastor are due also to the brethren who have so kindly and promptly forwarded their addresses, at his request, for publication. A. J. S.,
Deerfield Parsonage.

ORDER OF EXERCISES.

MORNING, 10:30 A. M.

Doxology.

Prayer.

Music.

Reading the Scriptures.

Singing—Hymn 573, C. M.

Historical Address by the Pastor, Rev. A. J. Snyder.

Singing—[An ode written by Mr. E. T. Taylor, of Wilmington, Del.] S. M.

> Hail! bright auspicious day,
> Hail! glad memorial hour,
> We come, with heart and voice to bless
> God's guarding, guiding power;
> With grateful, happy hearts,
> Our gladsome song we raise,
> Children, and children's children join
> Our father's, God to praise.
>
> We praise Thee, O our God,
> For what thy hand hath done;
> For garnered fruit within these walls,
> The trophies grace hath won.
> We bless Thee for the truth
> Proclaimed these many years;
> For the rich covenant of Thy love,
> Through sunshine and through tears."

Address by Rev. R. Hamill Davis, Ph. D., of Delaware, N. J. Subject—"Recollections."

Short address by Hon. Clifford Stanley Sims, of Mount Holly, N. J.

Singing—Hymn 594, C. M.

Benediction.

AFTERNOON, 3 P. M.

Music.

Prayer.

Address by Rev. Allen H. Brown, of Camden, N. J. Subject—"The Presbyterian Church in South Jersey, its Origin and Progress."

Singing—[A poem written by Rev. R. Hamill Davis for the Centennial of the Erection of this Church in 1871.] H. M.

"I love old Deerfield Church,
The church my fathers loved,
The church whose doctrines pure
These hundred years have proved;
And may she many a hundred more
In power and usefulness endure.

I love the dear old church;
To me 'tis dearer now
Than e'en cathedral grand,
With all its splendid show.
Far full a century has flown
Since rose its walls of solid stone.

I love the old, old church,
For sainted ones at rest
Worshipped devoutly here,
And now are with the blest.
Their memory sweet we cherish still,
And cherish it, we ever will.

I love, I love our church,
The birth-place of my soul;
And whereso'er I roam,
O'er earth from pole to pole,
No spot there'll be, more sweet to me,
Than this, I love so tenderly.

God bless old Deerfield Church,
Protect from every foe;
Nurtured of God, may she
To large proportions grow;
Till time itself shall cease to be,
Lost in a vast eternity."

Address by Caleb Allen, A. B., Principal of the W. J. Academy. Subject—"Important Events of the past 150 years."

Singing—Hymn 577, S. P. M.

Short address by Rev. Robert J. Burtt, of Marksboro, N.J.

Address by Mr. C. S. Tyler, of Greenwich, N. J.

Music.

Benediction.

EVENING, 7:30 P. M.

Music.

Reading of the Scriptures.

Prayer.

Singing—Hymn 944, P. M.

Address by Rev. James D. Hunter, of Greencastle, Pa. Subject—"The Sabbath School, its History and Work.

Singing—Hymn 575, S. M.

Address by Rev. David M. James, of Bath, Pa.

Address by Rev. William H. James, D. D., of Springdale, Ohio.

Singing.

Address by Rev. F. R. Brace, of Blackwoodtown, N. J. Subject—"The Church, and why we should love it."

Singing—Hymn 597, S. M.

Benediction.

HISTORICAL ADDRESS

BY THE PASTOR, REV. A. J. SNYDER.

PSALM 92: 14. "THEY SHALL STILL BRING FORTH FRUIT IN OLD
AGE; THEY SHALL BE FAT AND FLOURISHING."

In the introduction of the services of this anniversary occasion, we extend to you all a cordial greeting. Your presence
is an indication of the interest you have in this old historic
church, now having obtained its one hundred and fiftieth
birthday. We give you a hearty welcome, and are glad that
you have come to take part in these memorial exercises. Our
prayer is that the Great Head of the Church may be with us in
wonderful power, and bring a rich blessing to all our hearts.
Very naturally the preparation of a history of this church at
such a time as this would be laid at the door of the pastor; but
I would much rather the responsibility should have fallen into
other hands, better qualified for such an important task. Some
one has said that that nation is the happiest that has no history.
This may be true in regard to nations, and yet I doubt it,
especially in regard to Christian nations. But this truly cannot
apply to the church. We rejoice to-day that we have a history—a history of which we need not be ashamed. Like our
aged fathers and mothers, with children and grand-children and
great grand-children gathered around them, love to interest
them with stories of olden times, and talk of the scenes of their
early childhood, and of the many changes time has wrought all
along their pathway through life: so we to-day, gathered about
this hallowed spot, where so many precious memories cluster,
to celebrate the birth of this church, take pleasure in looking back to the days of its childhood and early religious experience, when the word of the Lord was so precious to God's
people, and note the changes God has wrought among His children, and the many blessings He has scattered all along their
pathway. Surely the Lord hath done great things for us, whereof

we are glad. Your presence here to-day from far and near, as children and friends of the "Dear old church," as it is sometimes called, is an evidence of your attachment to the church of your forefathers and your love for Zion. Truly you can say:

"I love thy Kingdom Lord!
The House of thine abode,
The Church our blest Redeemer saved
With His own precious blood."

I am not a little embarrassed in my preparations for this day's exercises to find that a history of this church was written about sixteen years ago by one of my predecessors, the Rev. R. Hamill Davis, Ph. D. In order to preserve and combine all the links of the golden chain of the church's history, my remarks must necessarily be in part at least a reproduction of the past history. Owing to the meagre records of the church's early history, (some of which are entirely lost), it would be impossible to give a full and complete statement of facts. As near as can be ascertained the organization of this church was effected between the years 1732 and 1737. The probability is that it occurred in 1737.

For about nine years the infant church had no regular pastor to break unto them the bread of life. But during all those years the gentle voice of the Great Shepherd and Bishop of Souls could be heard saying, "Fear not little flock, for it is your Father's good pleasure to give you the kingdom." The promise was fulfilled, and the kingdom came in mighty power. During this period, in the mysterious providence of God, the Master sent some of the choicest preachers of the word to minister to the spiritual needs of the people, such as Revs. Samuel Blair, Gilbert Tennent, Samuel Finley, perhaps Whitefield, and others. The Spirit of God was shed down in great abundance and the labors of those men of God were signally blessed. The awakening was widespread among the people, and the little church just born waxed stronger under the gracious visitation of Divine Providence, until it was encouraged and prepared to call its first pastor. We may safely say "Jehovah, Jirah," (The Lord will provide). In the darkest hour He leaves not, nor forsakes His people.

With such a starting point as this; with such tokens of the Divine presence and rich blessing at the very beginning of the church's life, is it surprising that we should have such a volume of interesting facts comprising the 150 years of the church's existence? Frequently do we find this church in the past to have been without an under-shepherd to minister regu. larly to the spiritual wants of the people, even for several years at a time; and yet the fostering and preserving care of our Heavenly Father sustained and perpetuated the existence of the church. Surely in those days there was ample room for the exercise of faith and patience, and those early settlers and early christians seemed to know how to endure hardness as good soldiers of Jesus Christ.

My text implies and teaches that the individual christian and the church in her organized capacity are productive of fruit—the fruit of holiness—in all ages of their experience; from youth to old age. No doubt this church, whose history we love and cherish, is a branch of that tree whose seed was planted on the eastern shore of Maryland by Rev. Francis Makamie, many years ago, and whose branches, like the Cedars of Lebanon, have spread, not only across Delaware Bay, but over this entire national domain.

The history of a church is largely made up of its ministry. About a score of pastors and stated supplies have labored in this part of the vineyard of the Lord during these 150 years, the most of whom have been faithful co-workers with the Master, and workmen that needed not to be ashamed.

As early as the year 1738 the Rev. Daniel Buckingham supplied the pulpit, and preached also at Pittsgrove. It was not long before the people of Pittsgrove expressed the desire to have a separate organization, and after some contention the Presbytery granted their request on condition that their house of worship should be six miles distant from the Deerfield church building.

The Rev. Andrew Hunter was the first on the list of pastors in the Deerfield Church. He was ordained and installed September 4th, 1746. He had acceptably supplied the pulpit for some time before his installation. He became pastor of the Greenwich Presbyterian Church at the same time, and continued his laborious labors in the joint charge until the year 1760, giving only one-third of his time to Deerfield. At this period his labors ceased in Deerfield, but he continued his work in the Greenwich Church until his death, which occurred July 28th, 1775. His sleeping dust reposes in the Greenwich burying ground. Tradition represents Rev. Andrew Hunter, the first pastor of the church, standing among his people with a leathern girdle around his tall form, dilating the truths in his most fervent passion; his large eyes emitting magnetic flashes, that held in wonder, fear and amazement the most stupid listener. He seemed to them like the risen personification of the Great Apostle of the Gentiles. It is said he would step from the platform and walk down the aisle among the congregation at the close of the service, raise the little children in his arms and bless them, and lay his hands on the heads of stalwart men and bless them; while his exhortations, so full of touching pathos for the welfare of others, shed a holy influence on all present.

After Mr. Hunter's resignation, as near as we can learn, the church was without a regular ministry for about four years. Then followed the Rev. Simon Williams in 1764; whether installed or not we cannot tell. He continued his labors in this field only about two years. The impression is that his short ministry was abundantly blessed, and the church greatly strengthened. From what we can glean he must have been a man of remarkable courage in rebuking sin among his people, and this may account for his short stay in this charge. Plain practical preaching, and faithfully rebuking sin, have made many short pastorates, and unsettled many devoted ministers of the gospel. John the Baptist was imprisoned for it, and finally sacrificed his life.

Mr. Williams was succeeded by the Rev. Enoch Green, who was installed pastor of the church June 9th, 1767. His ministry extended over a period of nine years, during which thirteen were added to the church. He is said to have been a man of good intellect and a splendid education. In connection with his pastoral duties he sustained a somewhat celebrated classical school in the old brick parsonage near the stream. The effect of this school was to fit and qualify a number of young men to go out into the world to fill positions of eminence and usefulness, and do their part well in the great drama of life. Mr. Green finished his work on earth in this field, falling asleep in Jesus December 2d, 1776. His remains lie buried beneath the church, with a marble slab to mark the spot, which was the gift of Dr. J. Barron Potter, of Bridgeton, N. J. The inscription on his tombstone, which lies on the eastern side of the church building, should include the fact that his bones lie mouldering beneath the church. It would be a praiseworthy deed for this congregation to perform during this period of the church's history.

After Mr. Green's labors followed the Rev. John Brainerd, who took charge of the church in 1777. His settlement was during those revolutionary "times that tried men's souls," and it is doubtful, therefore, whether he was ever installed as pastor. He had spent his best days as a missionary among the Indians, having succeeded his brother David in that capacity. It is said that he always loved the Indians; which is confirmed by the fact that he labored long and faithfully among them for their spiritual welfare.

John Brainerd was the son of Hezekiah and Dorothy Brainerd. He was born in Haddam, in the state of Connecticut, in 1720. He graduated at Yale College in 1746 with honor. He was licensed to preach by the Presbytery of New York in 1747, and was ordained to the gospel ministry in February, 1748. He received his appointment as missionary to the Indians in New Jersey, to succeed his brother David, June 2d, 1748, from a society in Edinburgh, Scotland, called "The Honorable Society for propagating Christian Knowledge." It was really a Foreign Missionary Society. He was a man qualified to fill any high and important position in the church of Christ, but preferred to bury himself in the swamps and forests of New Jersey for a bare pittance; depriving himself of many of the comforts and conveniences of life to labor for the welfare and spiritual good of both the whites and Indians. He founded churches and raised money to secure buildings to shelter them. Nearly his whole life was given to this work, having labored about thirty years in Burlington county. His territory extended from the Raritan River southward, and from the Delaware

River to the ocean. Much of the harvest produced by the good seed he scattered, has been reaped by other hands. He was a true patriot and lover of his country. Having incited his countrymen to stand in defence of their rights and resist the tyranny and oppression of Great Britain, he so aroused the vengeance and indignation of the British and the Tories, and the Revolutionary war so crippled and interfered with his life-long chosen work that he was obliged to seek a safer place of residence and a quieter field of labor, and hence he came to Deerfield. Wherever he went his influence was felt for good. He lives in the memory of the good and pious to-day. I understand that the Presbyterian Church at Mount Holly, where he lived and labored so long, and which is now rebuilding their church edifice, purpose to put in a Brainerd memorial window to perpetuate his memory. May God bless them for this deserving tribute of respect.

He was noted as a preacher of the gospel; he was eminent for piety; and after four years of faithful service in this church, he ceased from his labors and his works did follow him. He died much lamented. His remains also lie beneath the church, and a marble slab marks the spot, which is likewise the gift of Dr. Potter. This congregation could pay no higher tribute of respect, perhaps, to this departed saint, than to lay a marble slab on the outside of this building beside the Rev. Enoch Green's, his most intimate friend, inscribing upon it the fact that his remains are deposited on the inside, and so informing the passer by of future generations that his lifeless body reposes in this portion of the city of the dead.

The pulpit was now supplied for a season by Rev. Joseph Montgomery and others.

On the 25th day of June, 1783, the Rev. Simeon Hyde was ordained and installed pastor. After only seven weeks of earnest and successful effort in the Christian ministry, in the bloom and vigor of his young manhood, with brilliant prospects looming up before him, he was called to his reward on high. His body lies entombed in this yard to await the resurrection morn. In view of this sudden and unexpected loss to the church, we would say with the poet:

"God moves in a mysterious way
His wonders to perform;
He plants his footsteps in the sea,
And rides upon the storm.

For another period of about three years the church depended on supplies. On the 20th day of June, 1786, Mr. William Pickles was installed. By birth he was an Englishman. In the pulpit he was eloquent, but in his life inconsistent. The irregularities of his life soon excited a holy indignation in the minds of his people, who loved a pure gospel and an exemplary life; and hence, Mr. Pickles soon discovered that his room would be better appreciated than his presence. Having disgraced his profession, according to the account, his labors must have been brought speedily to a close in this charge, casting a dark shadow over this people, whom God had formed for himself. No doubt the church suffered greatly from Mr. Pickles' ministry. It is difficult to wipe out the stains and obliterate the influence of such a record as his. From this time the church was left eight years without a regular pastor; yet not entirely without the bread of life, for we learn that the pulpit was supplied at different times by different ministers. The dark clouds following each other in rapid succession, must naturally have reduced the church to a low condition, and left the little flock in a state of discouragement. But in all these years of trial, they were not left without the presence of God and the fulfillment of his precious promises. In His own good time and way He raised up for them, and for their comfort and encouragement, a good and excellent man in the person of Rev. John Davenport, who was installed pastor August 12th, 1795. He was a Jerseyman by birth; born at Freehold in 1752, and graduated at Princeton College in 1769. He labored for a number of years in other parts of the vineyard of the Lord before coming to Deerfield to care for this needy people. During his ministry more care must have been taken in preserving the records of the church. The first roll of church members appears in his time, June 6th, 1801. The membership then numbered eighty-five. Sixty-four persons were gathered into the church during his ministry of about ten years; years of faithful labor, rewarded by a plentiful harvest of souls. The darkness gave place to the light, and the light must have been sweet. The health of Mr. Davenport giving way, he withdrew from the charge October 16th, 1805.

After Mr. Davenport left, the church was again without an under-shepherd for the space of three years.

On October 20th, 1808, the Rev. Nathaniel Reeve was installed pastor, having come from Long Island to this charge. At one time he practiced medicine in Western Virginia. Fifty-two persons were added to the church as the fruit of his ministry. We are informed that the accessions were gradual; new additions at nearly every communion season, which is worthy of mention. Mr. Reeve resigned April 17th, 1817, after having served the church between eight and nine years.

Again the church was left without a pastor for more than two years. Then followed the Rev. Francis S. Ballentine, who was installed pastor June 22d, 1819. About the beginning of Mr. Ballentine's ministry there had been a general spiritual deadness prevailing in the church for some time, which was greatly lamented by the session. Although perplexed, yet not in despair, they resolved to pray for Zion still, and after patient waiting for about three years, with few accessions to the fold of Christ, showers of divine blessing came down upon the people. On December 6th, 1822, thirty-one persons sat down to the Lord's table for the first time, to enjoy the blessings of divine grace with God's redeemed people. Sixty persons were added to the church during Mr. Ballentine's labors, which is no mean record or showing for five years' service. A new church roll was made out shortly before he left this field, making the number of members one hundred and four. He resigned this charge June 8th, 1824, having been released at an adjourned meeting of the Presbytery of Philadelphia.

Another vacancy now occurred covering nearly two years, after which the Rev. Alexander McFarland was ordained and installed pastor of the church April 27th, 1826. His pastorate continued only four years, when he was called to a professorship in Dickinson College, Carlisle, Pa. It is said that he was a thorough Presbyterian and a fine scholar. He was succeeded by the Rev. John Burtt, who simply served as a supply for a brief period. During the short time he served the church, the Master gave him seals to his ministry, and a number were added to believers. After a time he was settled at Blackwoodtown.

He was followed by the Rev. G. D. McCuenn, who, having supplied the pulpit for six months, was installed pastor November 9th, 1831. About the time he entered upon his labors the membership numbered only seventy-seven. This slow growth in the church may be attributed, perhaps, to many, and sometimes long vacancies in the pulpit, and frequent changes of pastors. Such occurrences seem to militate against the prosperity of Zion. Mr. McCuenn's pastorate continued about five years. He received forty-one into the fold, and when his labors closed he left a membership of about one hundred. Again the church is left without a pastor.

The next on the list is the Rev. Benjamin Tyler, who was invited to supply the church for six months, but at the expiration of three months the congregation extended him a call to become their pastor, which was accepted. He was ordained and installed October 18th, 1837. He was born and raised at Greenwich, under the influence of the Society of Friends. Through the instrumentality of the Rev. Samuel Lawrence, he was led to make a profession of his faith in Christ. Twenty-three were added to the church during his ministry, but failing health made it necessary for him to seek a dissolution of the pastoral relation, which was obtained February 19th, 1842. He retired to Greenwich, where he died June 26th, 1842, and where his remains are interred. He was 37 years of age.

The Rev. Jacob W. E. Kerr followed Mr. Tyler. He was installed August 16th, 1842. He hailed from the Eastern Shore of Maryland, where Presbyterianism was first established in this country. His best years were devoted to this field. Both able and faithful, his ministry was owned and blessed. Some precious seasons were enjoyed, and frequent accessions to the church were made, but these were followed by seasons of spiritual dearth, and a low state of religion was greatly lamented by the most devout portion of the congregation. However, the people fasted and prayed and continued to make supplication until the windows of Heaven were opened, and a rich harvest of souls were gathered in. We learn that in December, 1845, thirty-one sat down to the table of the Lord for the first time. Ninety-seven were received during his ministry, which calls for profound gratitude. But it is not all sunshine here, for the painful duty was assigned him of laying five elders in the grave during his pastorate in this church. He was released from the charge by the Presbytery, May 1st, 1855. After this his time was occupied in supplying vacant fields. He died August 12th, 1879, aged 65 years, 7 months and 20 days, and his remains repose by the side of his companion in this old church yard, on the eastern side of the church building.

Mr. Kerr was succeeded by the Rev. Thomas W. Cattell, Ph. D., who was installed pastor of this church October 9th, 1855. He is represented as an earnest and zealous laborer in the vineyard of the Lord. Under his ministry professing christians were built up in holiness, and sinners yielded their hearts to God. Forty-eight persons united with the church during his labors here. Thirty-two of these were brought in in the year 1858, which was a period of special religious interest among so many of the churches.

In his time the church numbered about one hundred and thirty-five members. From the beginning, so far as the records show, about four hundred had been added to the church. His pastoral relation with this church was dissolved February 9th, 1860. From here he went to Princeton, N. J., and was principal and teacher in the Edgehill Academy until 1869. He then moved his school to Merchantville, N. J., and remained there until April, 1872, when he accepted the position as Professor of Mathematics in Lincoln University, Chester county, Pa., where he did a noble and self-denying work in preparing young colored men to labor for the elevation of the colored portion of the race. He closed his labors on earth in that institution, after having filled the position for about fifteen years. His death occurred June 29th, 1887, when about 64 years of age. His remains were entombed in Laurel Hill Cemetery, Philadelphia, on the 2d of July, 1887. He leaves a widow and six children to mourn his departure.

At the beginning of the preparations for this anniversary,

the hope was cherished that he would be with us to-day and take a prominent part in these services. The invitation was extended, but the condition of his health was such that he did not feel justified to make the promise. At that time he may not have realized that his end was so near at hand; but, alas! he, too, has gone. Another reminder that this world is not our home. How closely the messenger of death is following in the path of the laborers of this field.

The name of the next to follow on the list of pastors is as familiar to you as household words—I mean the Rev. R. Hamill Davis, Ph. D., whose memory is widely cherished in this congregation. He was much esteemed as a christian gentleman, and beloved as a pastor. Faithful to his calling and professional duties, the Lord added many seals to his ministry. About one hundred and ninety-four persons were received into the church as the fruit of his labors. Forty-two professed Christ at one time in March, 1868. Mr. Davis was born at Coatesville, Pa., March 25th, 1832. He was descended on his father's side from a Welsh and Swedish ancestry, but is Scotch-Irish through the ancestry of his mother. His grandfather, John Davis, served as an officer all through the Revolutionary war. His great grandfather, John Horton, was a signer of the Declaration of Independence, and gave the casting vote for Pennsylvania in the Continental Congress. Rev. Mr. Davis graduated at Lafayette College in 1852. After this he taught at the Lawrenceville school for four years. He studied Theology in Princeton Seminary, where he graduated in 1859. He was licensed to preach the gospel April, 1858, by the Presbytery of New Brunswick. He came to this church in August, 1860, which he supplied regularly until June 4th, 1861, when he was ordained and installed its pastor. The Rev. E. P. Shields, Rev. Samuel B. Jones, D. D., Rev. Joseph W. Hubbard, and the Rev. Samuel J. Baird, D. D., took part in the ordination and installation services. The pastoral relation was dissolved August 1875; a loving and appreciative people reluctantly consenting to the dissolution of the relationship so long sustained. He left Deerfield to become the principal of the Young Ladies Seminary at Lawrenceville, N. J. He retired from that position in 1883, with health greatly impaired.

On the restoration of his health he became the pastor of the Presbyterian Church at Delaware, N. J., in June, 1885, where he still labors to bless souls. Mr. Davis has the honor of having the longest pastorate here of any of his predecessors or successors; his labors covering a period of fifteen years. He was settled here during a very stormy period of the country's history. He commenced his pastoral work just about the time of the outbreak of the rebellion, when the entire country became unsettled and quivered from the centre to the circumference. By pursuing a prudent and consistent course he maintained his position well during all those years of civil warfare, when such a diversity of sentiment prevailed North and South, and when so many of our ministerial brethren became unsettled, either because they manifested too great loyalty to the government, or exhibited too much sympathy for the rebels. He is the author also of a carefully prepared history of the church up to the year 1871, which he read on the occasion of the celebration of the Centennial of Deerfield Church Building; an occasion which is looked back to by this congregation with a great deal of pleasure.

The history was afterwards published in pamphlet form, and may be found in the homes of many of this congregation. It is a valuable production, and should be preserved for future reference.

The following poem, composed by Mr. Davis and read by him on the centennial occasion, does not appear in the printed history, and considering it too good to drop out of sight, I obtained permission to use it on this occasion. It reads as follows:

"I love old Deerfield Church,
The church my fathers loved,
The church whose doctrines pure
These hundred years have proved;
And may she many a hundred more
In power and usefulness endure.

I love the dear old church;
To me 'tis dearer now
Than e'en cathedral grand,
With all its splendid show.

Far full a century has flown
Since rose its walls of solid stone.

I love the old, old church,
For sainted ones at rest
Worshipped devoutly here,
And now are with the blest.
Their memory sweet we cherish still,
And cherish it, we ever will.

I love, I love our church,
The birth-place of my soul;
And whereso'er I roam,
O'er earth from pole to pole,
No spot there'll be, more sweet to me,
Than this, I love so tenderly.

God bless old Deerfield Church,
Protect from every foe;
Nurtured of God, may she
To large proportions grow;
Till time itself shall cease to be,
Lost in a vast eternity."

Not only did Mr. Davis love the "dear old church," but he loved his home in the old parsonage, (as we now call it), where all his children were born; yes, he loves it still.

The Rev. W. H. Dinsmore was Mr. Davis' successor. He was installed pastor of the church March 15th, 1876. The Rev. L. E. Coyle, Rev. J. A. Maxwell, and the Rev. J. R. Wilson conducted the installation services. He came to this charge from Stroudsburg, Pa., where he had spent about five years of his ministerial life. After having been in this field about fourteen months—four of which he was laid aside from active duty—the Master called him to his eternal rest May 26th, 1878. His remains were interred at Phillipsburg, N. J. This was a sad bereavement to the church, for they highly esteemed and loved their newly chosen pastor, with whom they were called to part so soon. He left a widow and two children to mourn their loss, who reside near the resting place of his mortal remains. Nine persons were added to the church during his ministry. His two sons found the Saviour during the past year, and entered into covenant with God and His people, which is a great comfort to their mother.

He graduated from Princeton College in 1857, and from Princeton Seminary in 1860. In 1861 he was ordained and installed pastor of the Silvers' Spring Church, near Harrisburg, by the Presbytery of Carlisle. He left that church in 1865, and went to Mahanoy City, where he remained until 1869; going from there to Stroudsburg, and from there he came to Deerfield. He lived as he preached. He was a man of much earnest prayer, and wherever he worked was attended by marked revivals, and many were converted under his ministry. This church loved him and were wonderfully kind to him in his affliction. Nothing was left undone that could be done; but the Master called, and he must obey the summons.

On October 9th, 1877, a call was extended to the Rev. Edward P. Heberton, which he accepted the 22d of October following, and entered upon his duties as pastor elect October 28th, 1877. The installation took place April 1st, 1878. The committee appointed by Presbytery to discharge this duty were Rev. William A. Ferguson, the Rev. R. H. Davis, and the Rev. E. P. Shields.

Mr. Heberton graduated from Princeton, N. J., and was ordained to the gospel ministry in 1868 by the Philadelphia Presbytery. During his ministerial life he served the Great Valley Church in Chester county, Pa.; the Church of Duluth, Minn.; the First Church of Columbus, Ohio, and the Kenderton Presbyterian Church, of Philadelphia. He died in Florida in 1883, where he had gone for his health. He is spoken of as a man of rare abilities and an able preacher. He left a widow and five children to lament their sad loss, who at present reside in the city of Bridgeton, N. J. Twenty-one persons were added to the church during his ministry. The roll of members at the close of his labors was one hundred and ninety-seven, independent of those on the reserved list. His father also spent his life in the ministry, and is now about 84 years of age, honorably retired, and living in Philadelphia. His brother William likewise entered the ministry, and was ordained in 1869. His first charge was the Church of the Forks of Brandywine, Pa., and the second was Elkton, Md. He is now Treasurer of the Board of Ministerial Relief.

Mr. Heberton was succeeded by the Rev. James D. Hunter, who was called to this church in the fall of 1880. He was ordained and installed pastor of this charge November 30th, 1880. Those taking part in the services were Rev. H. L. Mayers, Rev. Heber H. Beadle, Rev. H. E. Thomas, and Rev. Frank E. Miller, of Easton, Pa., by invitation. He graduated at Lafayette College in 1878; entered Union Theological Seminary, N. Y., the same year, and was licensed to preach by the Presbytery of Lehigh, June 16th, 1880.

During the first year of his ministry here, it pleased the Lord to pour out of His spirit most copiously upon the people, and a precious revival of religion followed. The extra services were continued for some considerable time, and the religious feeling that prevailed was intense. As the result of this special spiritual interest, sixty-six professed Christ before the world, and sat down to the table of the Lord for the first time. His ministry continued about three years, in which he received eighty-three into the church as the fruit of his labors. He was zealously affected in every good work, which he prosecuted conscientiously and with commendable persistency. He resigned this pastorate in November, 1883, to accept a call to the Presbyterian Church of Greencastle, Pa., in the Presbytery of Carlisle.

He began his ministry at Greencastle, in December, 1883, and was installed in April, 1884. Mr. Hunter preached an historical sermon in 1884, on the occasion of the celebration of the Centennial of Franklin county, Pa., which was afterwards published in the "Greencastle Church, in Franklin county." He is still laboring in the same charge with encouragement and success.

A call was extended to your present pastor March 26th, 1884, and accepted by him April 13th, 1884. He and his family moved into what is called the old parsonage, April 25th, 1884. The congregation kindly and generously defrayed the expense of moving the furniture, which amounted to $20. The installation took place October 28th, 1884, the Rev. H. H. Beadle, Rev. L. E. Coyle and Rev. Wm. V. Louderbough, conducting the services. By these figures it will be seen that a trifle over three years have elapsed since I came among you. The record must necessarily be a very short one. Eighteen persons were admitted into the church during the above period. This is not a very flattering exhibit of ingathering, but there is something more to be done by God's ministers besides gathering in the sheaves. One part of a ministers duty is to labor to build up God's people in holiness, and fit them for the responsible duties of life. I soon discovered on entering on my duties in this field that the condition of things and circumstances were such as not to warrant the indulgence of a hope for early and rapid growth, and large accessions to the fold of Christ. Old sores must be healed; into the wounds existing the oil of gospel grace must be poured; and the alienated must be brought together in love and friendship. To this work of establishing peace and harmony the present incumbent addressed and applied himself. The hope is now cherished that the object in a great measure has been accomplished; that peace, and union, and harmony, now prevail throughout our borders. If this be so, may we not then indulge the hope that in the near future the Lord has a rich blessing to bestow; that by fervent prayer, an abiding faith, and earnest and faithful preaching of the word, this *old Tree*, which we trust is of God's own right hand planting, will yield an abundance of fruit, only the riper and better for the delay! The present roll of members is two hundred and fifty-six, including those on the reserved list. During my brief ministry here twenty-three marriages have been solemnized, and the parties entering into holy wedlock, sent on their way rejoicing. I also officiated at twenty-four funerals. But I must hasten on. A certain historian says, that no one can speak long of himself without being egotistical.

Of all the ministerial laborers connected with the history of this old historic church, only two remain to-day to join with us in these anniversary services. The rest have all laid their armour by to dwell, as we trust, at peace with God. This is a faithful reminder, that we who survive this little army of noble soldiers of the cross, must soon succumb to the inevitable, and likewise fall on the battle-field of life.

We must leave our history to be written by those who shall follow us, and take up the work where we left off. As we have been faithful to those who went before us, so they will do us justice when our bones lie mouldering in the dust.

In glancing over the many ministerial changes which have occurred during these 150 years, and observing that there was but one pastorate that reached fifteen years, the conclusion is arrived at that the outlook for the present pastor is not very flattering; or does not predict a very lengthy pastorate. Who knows but there may be some one already at work in this congregation digging his grave to bury him to make room for his successor! But let us hope for better things. Why indulge in a subject so sad and gloomy as this to-day—our happy Anniversary?

In glancing over the past, we notice that all the ministerial laborers of this charge have been called from other parts of the vineyard of the Lord; perhaps fulfilling the saying that "a prophet is not without honor, save in his own country."

But this church has not only been a receiver, enjoying the benefits of other mens' labors and talents; she has been likewise a producer; furnishing to the church at large talented men for the pulpit, and earnest workers for the pew.

The Rev. David M. James, pastor of the Presbyterian Church at Bath, Pa., and his brother the Rev. Wm. H. James, D. D., pastor of the Presbyterian Church at Springdale, Ohio, and also the Rev. John F. Sheppard, pastor of the Presbyterian Church at South Easton, are among those who have received their earliest religious impressions in this church, combined with good home influences; and have gone out from among us to prepare for the gospel ministry, and have entered important and useful fields of labor, where they are doing a good work for the Master in their ministerial calling.

The Rev. David M. James has long been in the ministry, and is at present occupying his second field of labor only, which speaks exceedingly well for his wearing qualities. His brother, the Rev. Wm. H. James, D. D., has been twenty-one years in his present charge, which has been his first and only pastoral charge. His people very thoughtfully celebrated his 20th anniversary among them, at which time he and his wife were made the recipients of some handsome presents as an expression of appreciation of his labors.

The Rev. John F. Sheppard was ordained by the Presbytery of Lehigh, in the synod of Pennsylvania, June 20th, 1881, and has been pastor of the Presbyterian Church at South Easton ever since.

Mr. John Dunlap, who has recently graduated at Yale, and completed his theological studies, preparatory to the gospel ministry, although a member of the Woodstown Presbyterian Church, N. J., his parents and brother belong to this part of the family of Christ. With rare natural endowments and a liberal education, his prospects for extensive usefulness are very good.

I learn also that the Rev. Robert P. DuBois, now deceased, but for many years pastor of the Presbyterian Church at New London, within the bounds of the Presbytery of Chester, Pa., was the son of Mr. Uriah DuBois, who at one time taught school in the district school house just above this church. Dr. F. L. DuBois, in Bridgeton, N. J., who now fills an important position under the Government, is the son of Rev. Robert P., and grandson of Uriah. The Rev. Robert P. DuBois lived to a good and ripe old age. He was a useful man in his day and generation. He preached the gospel for many years, and was greatly beloved by the people of his charge at New London. His life and work are still fragrant in the memory of a grateful and appreciative people.

The following are the names of the Ruling Elders who have served this church, as far as I have been able to secure them, viz: John Garrison, Jeremiah Foster, Arthur Davis, Thomas Read, William Tullis, Ezekiel Foster, Recompense Leake, William Smith, John Stratton, William Garrison, Abner Smith, Joseph Moore, Ebenezer Lummis, Dr. Joseph Brewster, Nathaniel Diament, Ebenezer Harris, Ephraim Lummis, Noah Harris, Samuel Thompson, Jonathan Smith, Benjamin Davis, William Garrison, Broadway Davis, Elijah D. Riley, John More, John Davis, Ludlam Dare, Samuel Barker, Jeremiah Parvin, E. B. Davis, Archibald Shimp, David Paris, Aaron Padgett, Thomas Bowen, John Ott and Robert Peacock. These have all died, as we trust, in faith, and gone to join the four and twenty Elders that come around the throne of God and the Lamb, except E. B. Davis, David Paris, Aaron Padgett,* John Ott and Robert Peacock. The last four constitute the present session of the church. E. B. Davis is now living at Phillipsburg. He was ordained and installed an elder of this church December 16th, 1848.

Archibald Shimp and David Paris were ordained and installed elders of this church on the 21st of May, 1854. Mr. Shimp died September 3d, 1883, having magnified his office and served the church faithfully in this capacity for about twenty-nine years. Aaron Padgett and Thomas Bowen were ordained and installed elders of the church February 9th, 1862. Mr. Bowen died December 30th, 1879, having served the church in this capacity for over seventeen years with great acceptance. In the death of these brethren the church sustained a heavy loss. David Paris and Aaron Padgett have both filled the office with credit to themselves and with satisfaction to the congregation—the former for thirty-three years and the latter for twenty-five years. John Ott and Robert Peacock were ordained and installed elders of the church April 17th, 1881. Experience shows that the selection was a good one; possessing sufficient courage and zeal to meet all the responsibilities of the office, and yet modest withal. Long may their lives be spared to be a blessing to this church, and be pillars in the house of our God.

The Sabbath School of this church was first organized during Mr. Ballentine's ministry, on March 29th, 1820, in the District School House, a short distance above the church, with about sixty in attendance during the early part of its history. It was first called "The Sabbath School Society of Deerfield Street, No. 1, in the Sunday School Union of Cumberland County." It was at first sustained by obtaining subscribers for its support. It appears that the society was in connection during its early years, with a Sunday School Union of Cumberland County, to which they annually, for seven years, elected a representative and paid an annual fee of one dollar, and receiving in return certain privileges. Up to the year 1847 the school had been regularly held in the Union School House. Then it was removed to the gallery of the church, where it was con-

---

*Elder Aaron Padgett died Oct. 3d, 1887, about 78 years of age.

tinued until the present chapel was built, which it has occupied
ever since. Up to the year 1865 the school was in session only
through the six summer months of the year; since then the sessions have continued during the entire year.

The following are the names of the Superintendents from
the beginning of the school, viz: Samuel Thompson, Esq.,
Broadway Davis, Mark A. Peck, David O. Garrison, John
Davis, Elijah D. Riley, James Davis, Samuel Barker, Mr. Olm-
stead, Charles O. Garrison, E. S. Corey, Ephraim T. Corey,
Ephraim B. Davis, Ephraim Davis, David S. Finley, David
Paris, Archibald Shimp, Joseph L. Davis, Alfred Davis, Elmer
Biddle, Dr. Charles C. Phillips, James Dunlap and George D.
Davis; only twenty-three in all from 1820 to 1887—stretching
through sixty-seven years. It was at first the custom to elect
several Superintendents for the term, in order that they might
alternate in conducting the school, and make it more certain
to have a presiding officer in the event of absence. George D.
Davis is the present Superintendent, and James F. Moore his
assistant. The school is properly officered with a band of noble
and faithful teachers, who are untiring in their efforts to lead
the children and rising generation to the Saviour. The school
numbers at present about one hundred and thirty or more.
The outlook for growth and usefulness is very hopeful.

On the 30th of April, 1820, a Sabbath School was started
at the West Branch School House, numbering about eighty-five
scholars. John More was its first Superintendent, and served
at least in that capacity for twenty-five years. This was a
branch school—being in sympathy and aim with the church
school. It was carried on faithfully and successfully during
all these past years, until a few years ago it merged into the
Deerfield Church School, for the purpose of concentration of
christian effort.

The Harmony Sabbath School, held in the District School
House, about four miles distant from the church, which was
organized in 1845, is a union enterprise. David Long was its
first Superintendent. For some years past G. Wilbert Moore
and John Ott have served in that capacity—each presiding
during alternate years. It is made up of Presbyterians and
Lutherans. A number of our people are usefully employed on

Sabbath afternoons at that place, and are doing a noble and self-denying work for the Master. The school numbers about fifty-four. The average attendance is about forty-four. During the Rev. R. Hamill Davis' ministry the "Elfie Mission Band" was organized, August 14th, 1872, with twenty-four members; drawn principally from the Sabbath school or schools. It still has a living existence, and is doing a good work in aid of the Mission cause. Miss Ella F. Garrison was its first and much esteemed President. At present it is under the efficient supervision of Miss Belle Flanagan as President. Miss Mattie A. Biddle is Secretary, and Miss Lillie Ballenger is Treasurer. The band was named "Elfie"—called after a boat by that name, furnished the mission at Corisco, Africa, by the children of this country.

Under the same pastorate an "Auxiliary" to the "Woman's Foreign Missionary Society" was organized February 23d, 1872. The number of persons induced to become members the first year was about sixty. Notwithstanding deaths and removals have thinned their ranks, reducing their members to between thirty and forty, I believe they have never paid out less than $50 a year to the cause of Missions, except perhaps one year. No means is left untried to increase its membership, deepen the interest, and swell the contributions. With such a laudable object before the society as the salvation of the millions of heathen, and especially the elevation of their own sex, I bespeak for it a bright and prosperous future. Mrs. R. Hamill Davis was its first President. The present officers are: President, Mrs. Cordelia M. Richer; Secretary, Mrs. Rhoda D. Moore; Treasurer, Mrs. Sarah M. Ott.

There is in connection with the church also an "Aid Society," sometimes known as the "Church Sociable." The object of this association is to develop the social element of the congregation, and to raise funds by regular and small contributions for such uses and improvements as the circumstances and condition of the congregation may require. The fund raised is supplementary to the regular income of the church; and often comes to the relief of the church when embarrassed for the want of means. It accomplishes a good work, and ought to enlist the sympathies of the entire congregation. It was organized March 13th, 1878, in the early part of Mr. Heberton's ministry. The whole amount raised from 1878 to 1887, only nine years, is $875.58. From members fees, $249.98. From festivals, $621.82, and by cash, $3.78. The present officers consist of: President, Mrs. A. J. Snyder; Secretary, Miss Mattie A. Biddle; Treasurer, Mrs. Cordelia M. Richer.

Let us now take a brief survey of the church buildings, in which the congregations have worshipped, of which I have said nothing heretofore. Tradition says that in the year 1732 there came to this country from Scotland and the North of Ireland and from Germany, a small colony of Presbyterians, bringing their Bibles and catechisms in their trunks, and the Spirit of God in their hearts, and settled in what is now called Deerfield and Hopewell townships, then a wild wilderness, wooded with large timber and inhabited by Indians, with very little of the soil cleared. There was, however, a clearing not far from where this old stone church now stands, of some hundreds of acres of new land, and very fertile, on which the grass grew luxuriant, and the wild deer came out into this clearing in large numbers to feed, from which the place derived the name of Deerfield.* Those men distributed themselves; they bought land in different parts of those two townships, as it is now arranged, and erected their log houses; for there were no other kind in those days. And when they procured houses for their families, they met together and concluded to erect a building for a school house, and in which they might also hold religious services. In that building the people met together for worship, some of them coming a long distance, and taking their turns in bringing their tallow candles, with which to light up the house for the evening service. Whether they had a preacher at that time or not we cannot tell, but we do know that they met together for worship, and their numbers increased until the little log school house became too small. In the year 1737 they were

---

*Thomas Shourds' History and Genealogy of Fenwick's Colony says: About 1725 Benjamin Davis purchased 1000 acres of land in North Cohansey precinct of Dan. Cox, the great land speculator, a resident of Burleighton, for which he paid ten shillings per acre. The price which he paid Cox was considered by the inhabitants of the precinct VERY DEAR; hence they called it a DEARFIELD. Why the name has been changed to DEERFIELD I can't imagine. In after time that and other lands adjacent were set off as a township called DEERFIELD.

organized into a church, and resolved to erect a church building, which was known as the Log Church. They came with their ox teams, for they had no others. They cut down the cedars and carted them to the place designated for the building. And log after log was hewn and notched, and dove-tailed together, and at last there appeared the beautiful Log Church in the forest.* The fathers dedicated it to the worship of Almighty God, and named it the Deerfield Presbyterian Church. And for thirty-four years they worshipped in the old Log Church, which stood in the adjoining grave yard, a little south of the present church building. It has nothing to mark its location, except the grave of John Leake, which is said to be beneath or near the old pulpit, at his own request.

It would be a noble deed for the people of this generation worshipping here, to place a handsome monument over this grave, with suitable inscription upon it, which marks the spot where the old church stood, and where our ancestors worshipped. Although not a vestige of the old Log Church remains, yet the old Brittannia Communion Service, supposed to be the first used by our forefathers, out of which they ate and drank in commemoration of the dying love of Jesus, may be seen on the table in front of this platform to-day.† Some years ago a new service was secured, and the old service placed in the hands of Dr. J. Barron Potter, of Bridgeton, N. J., for preservation, and to prevent their use for common vessels.

If there is any reliance to be placed on tradition, the members of this church in its early history manifested a high appreciation of the gospel, and practiced great self-denial to hear it dispensed. Mr. Charles S. Tyler, son of the Rev. Benjamin Tyler, now deceased, but fifty years ago the pastor of this church, sends me the following: He says, "My mother has told me upon the authority of very old people in Deerfield, when she lived there, that a common way of getting to Greenwich church from Deerfield, with those that had horses, was to

---

*At this point a little Log Cabin was exhibited, made of the pith of corn stalks, to remind the congregation of the days of old, when their forefathers worshipped in the little Log Church.

†It was placed on the table on this occasion to exhibit for the gratification of the congregation assembled.

ride and hitch. Part of the family would start on foot, and afterwards another or more would mount the horse or horses and ride on ahead of the others and hitch, and walk on. The others, when they reached the horse or horses, would mount and ride forward; and so continue until they reached the church." He says, "A mode of church going unheard of by the majority of people at this time." The probability is that the Greenwich church was connected with Deerfield church in one charge at the time referred to—a distance of about ten miles.

I am credibly and reliably informed also, that mothers with their children, and others also, would walk the entire distance from Deerfield to Greenwich to a Sabbath morning service. In some instances they would carry their shoes and stockings until they had almost reached the place of worship; then they would stop and wash their feet in the little stream by the wayside, put on their shoes and stockings, and appear in the house of God as clean and tidy as their neighbors, who might be more highly favored with greater facilities for travel. But time has brought with it great changes. A single mile is now considered almost too long a distance to walk to the "place where God's honor dwelleth and His name is recorded." New modes of locomotion have been devised, making it far easier and more convenient to reach the house of God. New methods also for heating the sanctuary have been discovered; insomuch that the ancient foot stove, at one time used in this place of worship, has been dispensed with; a sample of which may be seen on this platform to-day.* In the face of all these facts, "Say not thou, what is the cause that the former days were better than these? for thou dost not inquire wisely concerning this."—Eccl. 7: 10.

The present church building was erected in 1771; or rather the building of which this is the enlargement. It was accomplished during the pastorate of the Rev. Enoch Green. Evidently the people struggled long and hard to secure their new church home. The edifice was 38 feet by 48 feet, with a curved

---

*One of those ancient foot-stoves was secured from one of the families of the church and placed on the platform on this occasion for the curiosity of the rising generation.

ceiling. In the course of some years it was remodeled inside, and a flat ceiling substituted in the place of the curved one. When the church was enlarged to its present size, the ceiling was curved again as we now see it, and according to its original form. In 1852 a new roof was put on the building. The addition to the church of 25 feet, with a recess of 7 feet for the pulpit, was made during the ministry of Rev. Thomas W. Cattell. On Monday morning, August 16th, 1858, the first stones were taken out of the end wall; the estimated cost was about $3,000. The building committee consisted of the Trustees of the church, and are as follows, viz: David Padgett, Ephraim B. Davis, Robert More, Lucius Moore and Arthur Davis.

Fortunately for the church, at this time she had an accumulated fund at interest of about $2,850, which was used to cover the expenses of enlargement and improvement. The fund referred to was obtained from the sale of timber from the eighty acres of woodland in possession of the church—property secured by our forefathers and handed down to us as a legacy for the use of religious purposes.

During the ministry of the Rev. James D. Hunter some extensive improvements were made, at a cost of from five to seven hundred dollars. The walls were newly frescoed, the wood-work painted, the pulpit changed, and the recess fitted up for the choir. In addition to this an old debt of three hundred dollars was cancelled about the same time.

During the present pastorate, near $300 was raised and expended on this building in making alterations and improvements—the people giving cheerfully and liberally. The floor of this church had never been carpeted, except the aisles and pulpit platform, until last spring, when the entire floor was covered over with a rich and beautiful carpet. At the same time the doors of the pews were removed, the pews re-numbered, and partitions placed beneath all the pews. There is another improvement that might be made, and which would add very much to the beauty of this ancient structure, and serve likewise a valuable purpose; I mean a suitable tower, with a sweet-toned bell hanging in it, to call the people to the house of God. This would not disturb the sleeping dead who repose in their dusty beds, but it might be instrumental in awakening some sleeping soul, and bringing to the enjoyment of spiritual life those who are dead in trespasses and sins.

The question of building a chapel to be used in connection with the Deerfield Presbyterian Church, was agitated as far back as the year 1858, when the Rev. Thomas W. Cattell was pastor, who recommended the starting of a fund to be used for that purpose. Nothing was accomplished in the way of getting a building until the year 1873, when a festival was held to establish a fund for the object in view. The money realized at the fair and festival was loaned out for a time, and when paid in the principal and interest amounted to $346. In the spring of 1878, the Rev. E. P. Heberton, (who was pastor at that time), agitated the matter, and at the annual meeting held April 27th, 1878, the following named gentlemen were appointed a committee to contract for and erect a suitable structure in which to hold Sabbath School, evening meetings, lectures, &c., viz: Rev. E. P Heberton, Edo O. Leake, Elmer Biddle, Moses Peacock, Sr., and Robert More. The Chapel was erected and is 30 feet by 50 feet, with 14 feet posts, and a vestibule 6½ feet in width. The contractors for the building were the firm of Conover & Ackley, of Bridgeton, N. J. The cost of the building was $1317; the cost of the furniture, including the blinds, was $324.40, making in all $1641.40. The two stoves included in the furniture were a present from Elmer Biddle, and cost $25. In addition to the above there are two organs used in the chapel; the cost of the larger one was $200, and the cost of the smaller one was $20. The Treasurer, Edo O. Leake, made this very cheering and satisfactory statement, he says: "When the building was finished it was all paid for and $10 left on hand." An unusual experience! Really, this is something new under the sun! But the most surprising thing is that this church did not avail herself of this great convenience many years sooner. I do not know that the treasurer of the church to-day can rejoice in a surplus, as in the case above; but I am happy to announce on this Anniversary occasion, that the church is entirely free of all debt. I apprehend that it has been characteristic of this church to guard against such inconveniences. Thirty dollars was expended last summer in painting the walls of the chapel to give them a more attractive appearance and better finish.

I almost failed to note that about the same time a neat chandelier, with three burners, was purchased and suspended from the arch of the recess of the church for the benefit of the choir and speaker; besides, six additional burners were secured for the main part of the audience room. The cost of the above improvement was about $20, and was paid by the Aid Society.

The Rev. Enoch Green was the first pastor who occupied a parsonage in this charge, or Deerfield Presbyterian Church. It consisted of fifty acres of land, with a brick house and other needed improvements. In the course of about fifty years, and during Mr. Ballentine's ministry, the brick house gave way to a frame building, well constructed, on a more beautiful site, and a little farther north of the stream. The building still stands, now over sixty years since its erection. This property was used as a parsonage, or home for the pastor of the church, until the present pastorate, when the subject of a change was extensively agitated throughout the congregation; most of them favored the change, and yet there were a few exceedingly loath to part with the old parsonage. They loved it—their souls, as it were, cleaved unto it. Like the Psalmist, when he said: "My soul cleaveth unto the dust."—Psalm 119: 25. And no wonder, it was a beautiful spot. It had been in possession of the church one hundred and thirty years, handed down to them by their forefathers, to be used for such a purpose. But the contemplated change did not imply alienation of the property; only that the proceeds of the farm be invested in another home, more suitable for the pastor in these times.

At a meeting of the congregation held August, 1884, it was decided, if the way be clear, to sell the farm and secure another property to be used as a parsonage, and the trustees of the church were appointed a committee to carry out the wishes of the congregation. The trustees at this time consisted of Enoch Riley, Edo O. Leake, George D. Davis, Daniel Padgett and Elijah R. Parvin. In a very short time about an acre of ground was purchased of Elijah R. Parvin, to be used for the purpose, for the sum of $400, situated in the southern part of the village of Deerfield. Arrangements were entered into at once to erect suitable buildings thereon. Mr. A. F. Randolph, of Bridgeton, N. J., contracted for the work, which was begun and carried on so speedily as to enable the present pastor to take possession on the 18th day of March, 1885. The old parsonage was sold at public sale on the 18th day of December, 1884, to Lewis M. Brooks, for $62 per acre, amounting to $3100; Mr. Charles Barker was the auctioneer. The new property cost, including the land, about $3,287.65, and is a convenient and very desirable place of residence; I may say it is a model home. To make up the deficiency to pay for the cost of the new property, a sufficient amount of timber was sold from the woodland to cover the additional expense; hence it is free from debt, and made so without burdening a single member of the congregation. One hundred dollars was added to the pastor's salary by a considerate people, who thoughtfully considered the shrinkage of his income by the change. I may add here, that ever since some time during Mr. Davis' ministry, only seven acres of the fifty in the farm were cultivated by the pastor, he wishing less care; the balance of the farm was used for the benefit of the church. It was not until the year 1810, during Rev. Nathaniel Reeve's ministry, that the church became an incorporated body, and a Board of Trustees was elected. Before this period the congregation appointed committees to attend to the temporalities of the church.

The present Board of Trustees consists of Daniel Padgett, Elijah R. Parvin, Charles D. Moore, Joseph L. Davis and G. Wilbert Moore; one trustee is elected annually to serve for five years. The present organist is Miss Anna P. Veal, who has served faithfully for the past three years. Her immediate predecessor was Miss Ella Moore, (now Mrs. Davis); she served for a short period of time and did her part well. Previous to this Miss Juliet Moore occupied the position for twelve years, and with great acceptance. Mr. Wm. Laning is the present efficient leader of the choir, and has filled that position for the past five or six years. Mr. Elijah R. Parvin was his predecessor, who held the position for sixteen years. His long continued and self-denying labors need no comment; they speak for themselves. For the past five years a musical committee appointed by the congregation, selects the members of the choir.

Elijah R. Parvin is the present sexton, and has occupied that position for the last fifteen years. During that period he has opened one hundred and forty-seven graves, and all but two in the yard on the eastern side of the street. His predecessor was Mr. David Ott.

In the early history of the church the salary of the sexton was only $6 a year, it has now reached $75 a year; and is still too limited for the amount of labor required.

If time and space would allow, we might speak of men born and reared in this community with large mental capacity and endowments, and who filled very important positions in this and other localities. But I cannot resist the temptation to refer to a few. The first I shall notice is Dr. Holmes Parvin. One of his successors, Dr. Charles C. Phillips, pays the following tribute of respect to him: In a Sabbath School address, delivered in 1876, he says, "Holmes Parvin, a name familiar to all, was born in this county December 7th, 1794. After receiving an English education, he attended the medical lectures in the University of Pennsylvania, where he graduated in 1815. He immediately commenced and continued to practice in this village until 1829, when he emigrated West, settling in 1830 in Cincinnatti, where he soon had an extensive practice, but which in 1836 he abandoned to give himself up to other pursuits; especially to investigate his favorite science of electricity. Long before Professor Morse's name had any connection with the telegraph, Dr. Parvin had commenced, and so far perfected his instruments as to communicate with adjoining rooms, and prophesied to his friends that the time would come when we, by electricity, would communicate with our most distant acquaintances. They thought him mad, but we of to-day see his prophecy verified. To continue his experiments and communicate his theories to scientific men, he removed in 1838 to Philadelphia, but his health soon failing, he removed again in 1840 to Cincinnatti, where he died February 6th, 1842, leaving two children, one of whom, Rev. Robert J. Parvin, an Episcopal Clergyman, recently perished in the flames of a burning steamer on the Ohio river." Dr. Parvin was intimately associated with the Sabbath School of this church.

Neither would this history be complete without making

allusion to such men as Col. David Moore and his son Dr. Samuel Moore. Mr. C. S. Tyler, of Greenwich, gives me the following information: He says, "From one of the oldest of the Deerfield families was descended Mary Seeley, wife of Rev. Mr. Tyler; her mother Elizabeth Moore, was the only daughter of Col. David Moore, an officer of artillery in the Continental Army, who, after recovering at home, where he was allowed to be nursed, from a grape shot wound received at the battle of Germantown, returned to the service of his country. During the dark night of September 18th, 1777, when over-confidence and wine had led General Wayne, at the Paoli Tavern, Chester county, into the neglect of duty, and enabled General Grey, of the British army, to surprise and massacre many of our forces, even after numbers of them had surrendered, Col. Moore, with Captain John Beaty, were the only ones that succeeded in saving a cannon from the hands of the enemy. And to his son, Dr. Samuel Moore, virtually belongs the honor of the famous Missouri compromise measure. Born in Deerfield February 8th, 1774, he graduated at the University of Pennsylvania in 1791, where he afterwards served as tutor. In 1796, after a thorough course of study, he graduated in medicine. After commencing the practice of his profession in Bucks County, Pennsylvania, his health failed; and by the advice of Dr. Rush he sailed for Canton, and with such happy results, that he afterwards made four other voyages to Canton, and one to Calcutta. In 1808 he settled permanently in Bucks County, where his upright life and remarkably winning manners joined to unobtrusive ability, gained him such influence among all classes, that in 1818, while absent upon business in the west, he was nominated by the Whigs and elected to Congress, and twice re-elected. In 1824 he was appointed by President Monroe, Director of the Mint, which office he continued to hold during the administration of Mr. Adams, and part of that of General Jackson, who refused to pay any attention to the many efforts made to displace him. When informed by Dr. Moore of his desire to leave the Mint, the President requested him to keep the matter a secret until a successor was selected, and asked Dr. Moore to name a suitable person for the office, when at his suggestion his brother-in-law, Dr. Patterson, was appointed, the public first learned of a contemplated change. Upon leaving that office he was honored with a complimentary testimonial of General Jackson's esteem.

It was owing mainly to his efforts that the appropriation from Congress was secured for the building of a new Mint, and under the immediate superintendence of Dr. Moore, that the present Mint on Chestnut street was erected, and the works removed from the old building on Seventh street. Dr. Moore retired from the Mint in 1835, and became President of the Hazleton Coal Company, which position he retained until the time of his death, February 18th, 1861. Although in his eighty-eighth year when he died, he seemed never to grow old through the loss of interest in knowledge in all its departments at home and abroad. At his death he and Professor Silliman of Yale College, were the oldest members of the American Philosophical Society.

It was during his service in Congress that the celebrated Missouri Controversy arose. In its settlement none took more interest than Dr. Moore, who was one of the select committee to whom the subject was referred. After the failure of all other efforts for peace, he suggested and presented to Mr. Clay, in the form of a resolution, the measure which that great statesman brought forward for the settlement of that controversy, and which was finally accepted February 27th, 1821. After the act was passed Mr. Clay, with highly complimentary remarks, handed the original draft to Dr. Moore, adding: "Take this paper home with you and preserve it for your children."

While a daughter could say of him, 'I never heard him say a foolish thing,' Dr. Moore was always attractive to old and young alike, as a companion, gentleman and christian. A man of whom any place might be proud as having given him birth."

But I must now draw my remarks to a close; pardon me for having wearied your patience and trespassed so long upon your time. In the limited time allotted me on this occasion, I could barely give an outline of the history of this part of God's Zion, which stretches over nearly five generations.

How rapidly we have passed the milestones to-day in our march along the line of the Church's History. We have observed one generation after another of workers pass away, while others have been raised up to fill their places; and so the work goes on in the midst of the many and serious changes. Rich and precious fruit have we been permitted to pluck to-day from this old tree, planted here one hundred and fifty years ago, whose roots strike deeper and deeper, and whose branches extend farther and farther, and which is destined to bring forth fruit in old age. The tall and large oaks of four score must decay and pass away, but the church will continue to be fat and flourishing—she will bring forth fruit in old age. Exposed both to fire and storm, this church building, or part of it, has stood for one hundred and sixteen years, and by God's protecting care may stand many more. But the church proper, in her organic form, has passed through many and severe forms of trial, and yet survived them all. Adverse circumstances have frequently overtaken her in her onward march; false and untrue friends have cast the shadows of discouragement and despondency across her pathway. Deaths and removals have thinned the ranks of the soldiers of the cross and weakened the forces of the workers in the vineyard, and yet the church has strengthened and increased with the increase of her years, as she comes up from the wilderness leaning upon her beloved.

When we consider that the church on earth and the church in heaven are one, then it is clearly to be seen that the church's loss on earth is but the church's gain in heaven. Truly says the poet:

"One family we dwell in Him,
One church above, beneath;
Though now divided by the stream,
The narrow stream of death.

One army of the living God,
To his command we bow;
Part of his host have crossed the flood,
And part are crossing now.

Ten thousand to their endless home
This solemn moment fly;
And we are to the margin come,
And we expect to die."

As we look back over the past to-day, we cannot fail to enumerate many scenes, both painful and joyous. We therefore mingle our tears of sorrow with our feelings of joy. You cannot fail to call to mind when death robbed you of some of the dearest earthly objects of your affection, and sorrow filled your heart. Every time you visit their graves a new pang of grief pierces your soul, but many and rich have been your experiences of joy also in your connection with the church here on earth. As you glance over the past you are able to recount at least some of God's dealings of love and mercy. You have had your seasons of refreshing from the presence of the Lord; our Heavenly Father has answered your prayers, and the Spirit of God has been poured out in copious showers, and your sons and daughters have come from afar, and been gathered into the fold of Christ; and when the bands that have bound you to earth have been snapped asunder, it has only been to multiply the ties in heaven. With all these rich blessings of the past, which have made us what we are, what is the future likely to be? From the past, I venture to judge the future will be still more glorious. I apprehend the church shall flourish like the palm tree, and grow like the cedars in Lebanon. She has kept pace with the progress of events, and with the developments of the arts and sciences; indeed she has been, with Christ as her head, at the bottom of all true science and development.

And now with these thousands of broad acres of fertile land surrounding this cherished spot, all dotted over with beautiful and convenient farms, occupied with an intelligent and God loving people, with increasing advantages for giving your children a liberal education, favored also with a faithful gospel ministry proclaiming the standards of the church in all their purity and simplicity, and with God's blessing resting upon your labors, I predict a still grander future for the church than the past; increased prosperity and liberality, a more thorough consecration to the work at home, and a more intense love and devotion to the work of saving the millions of heathen abroad.

However rich and grand the past has been, the future must necessarily be still more bright and hopeful, because the facilities for enlargement are increasing with the growth of years. Your most desirable pews are occupied and even crowded, and more are needed to supply the demand. The removals by death and otherwise cause no diminution in the size of our congregations.

A word of counsel from one who has already become warmly attached to this portion of the Lord's vineyard, I presume will not be considered as an intrusion. Fathers and mothers in Israel, young men and maidens, and also little children, let me urge upon you the necessity of loving your church; the church your fathers loved; it is the birth-place of your soul; let it be as

"Dear as the apple of thine eye,
And graven on thy hand."

Let your post of duty always be filled, "Whatsoever your hands find to do do it with all your might." Never fail to let your voice be heard in behalf of Zion; for her welfare let your prayers ascend; consecrate yourselves wholly to her service, but above all, love the Saviour who hath bought her with his own most precious blood. Then with the great apostle of the Gentiles shall we be able to "rejoice evermore." Therefore,

Joyful joyful let us be,
On this Anniversary Day;
Three times fifty are our years,
With no cause for shedding tears.

God has brought us safely through
All these years of trial too;
Having reached this good old age,
Adding now another page.

With the record of the past,
Showing so much of God's grace;
We can safely trust Him now,
And perform to Him our vow.

Let us then fresh courage take,
In God's work for Jesus' sake;
Trusting in the Saviour's love,
Till we all shall meet above.

THE STONE PRESBYTERIAN CHURCH OF DEERFIELD--ENLARGED IN 1859.

ADDRESS OF REV. R. HAMILL DAVIS.

Substance of an Address on Recollections of Deerfield
Presbyterian Church, by Rev. R. Hamill.
Davis, Ph. D.

It were a strange heart that beats within me, if it did not
beat faster here to-day; if, on this interesting historic occasion,
and amid these suggestive surroundings, I could stand before
you, without the throb of a more than ordinary emotion. Who
is there, of all this assembly, that does not feel the inspiration
of the hour? and who, among you, feels it more than I?

Your invitation to join you and take some part in these
exercises I gladly accepted. Your pastor has riveted your
attention, as he has traversed, so ably and so fully, this long
century and a half of years, in which God has protected and
prospered this venerable church. And now, giving myself up to
the past which we have had in common here, I propose to
indulge for a little while in the "Recollections" that it brings.
And how they come thronging upon me, at the bidding of busy
faithful memory!

In the line of pastors who have come and gone, I occupy
a *somewhat isolated* position. When I came to you, my two
immediate predecessors were at work in other fields. One of
them, the Rev. J. W. E. Kerr, now sleeps in the old church
yard, among your kindred, and the people to whom he faithfully and ably preached the gospel for many years. The other,
I hoped to meet here to-day, but only a few weeks ago death
came to the Rev. Dr. T. W. Cattell, in the midst of an active
and honorable service, and he too sleeps in the grave. One of
my two immediate successors, the Rev. W. H. Dinsmore, had
but fairly entered upon his work here, with promise of great
usefulness, when he was cut down, in your midst, by the hand
of death. The other, the Rev. E. P. Heberton, a man of
brilliant parts, whose monument is yonder chapel, not very long
after he left you found a grave in the sunny South. Now all
this seems to sound of the long ago, and yet it has not been

very many years since I first stepped on Deerfield soil; and though I stand before you, with the few stray locks that are left, already whitened, yet it is not the frost of life's Winter, but rather of the early Autumn that has touched them. But all this in passing, I am not a boy any longer, I felt more like that when I came to you, fresh from my scholastic life, an inexperienced young man, twenty-seven years ago. I had a great deal to learn, and I learned it; I left you a wiser man than I came. I wonder that you bore with me so kindly; it may be that my worst faults came first, and I corrected them as the years rolled on. I well remember my first visit; it was a gloomy day in April, 1860. The day gave color to my first impressions of Deerfield; but before I left I was drawn toward the people and the church and consented to repeat my visit. The next time it was a bright sunny day; the birds sang in the trees, the air was redolent with the fragrance of blossoms, and the fields were green. The people received me kindly, my heart warmed toward them, and I felt within me that if they called me I would come. They did call me, and I came.

Of those who then constituted the Presbytery of West Jersey, but one still answers to his name, the Rev. A. H. Brown, who well deserves to be called our "Ecclesiastical Historian" in New Jersey, and has been wisely chosen to take an important part in these exercises to-day.

Of the session that rallied around the new pastor, only one, my old neighbor, David Paris, remains.

And the congregation, O! the congregation! I see them still, as they were wont to appear in other days, but I look, in vain, among you now, for vanished forms that come not back again. There is scarcely a house in this whole congregation that Death has not entered since first I looked in upon the living ones. If we were to let the great Conqueror lead us along from home to home, at almost every door, he would grimly boast of his triumphs.

Then there are reminiscences of blessed memory that we gratefully recall to-day, times when the Spirit's presence was powerfully manifested among us; but, as a general fact, they kept gradually dropping into the fold, so that there were rarely two successive communion seasons without some additions to the church. Individual cases of peculiar interest come to my mind just now, but I cannot even allude to them here. It is a great pleasure, though not without its sadness, to go with you into this past, where we have so much in common. But it is not necessary to come back to Deerfield to have the reminiscences awakened. They have often come to me when far away, and if I should go to the ends of the earth, I would carry with me Deerfield, the old church, the old parsonage near the stream, and the old familiar forms and faces, on to the end of my pilgrimage. There are some memories that fade not with years; some photographs that no future can harm; some impressions that time cannot efface.

Just here, I know that you will pardon a very personal reminiscence. For nearly two years I lived among my people a bachelor, shy of the young ladies, fond of the little girls. One Sabbath I announced that I would be absent for a few weeks, and a good lady, as I passed down the aisle, playfully remarked, "I believe you are going to get married," and sure enough, it was not long before I brought from the city a young inexperienced maiden, whom I have ever since been proud to call my wife; and so it is to me a happy circumstance, that our "silver wedding" coincides with the one hundred and fiftieth anniversary of the old church. And there could be no better place and time for me to testify, that if God has made me useful and happy here, or anywhere, it is due in the largest measure, to the true wife, who alike in sunshine and under the clouds, has stood faithfully at my side, and who comes back to-day with a heart that warms to you as to no other people on the face of the earth, our first church love, and the old Parsonage, where all our birdlings were nestled. Is it any wonder that it still has to us the charm with which only such associations can invest it? We left with the nest unbroken, but some of you remember the fair little blue-eyed girl, who spent seven bright summers among you, and used to play under the willows; she and her sister were the last of the little girls that played under those willows before the woodman's axe cut them down, and *she* now lives where the angels live.

But time passes on, and we must drop these reminiscences. Some day in that wonderful 20th century, of whose dawn we already catch somewhat the first glimmering light, the people will come, we trust, as we come to-day, to the two hundredth anniversary of the old church of Deerfield, but we shall not be here. Some of these children will still be this side the River, but most of us will be over on the other shore. What the great developments of the world's history are to be the next fifty years we cannot tell, God only knows. In the shaping of that history, among the vast multitudes of Earth, but little, comparatively, depends on what your hands may find to do—but not so with this old church of your fathers. Whether the men and women of Deerfield in 1937 are to hang their harps upon the willows, and weep when they remember Zion, or take their harps and touch the cords, and make the air vocal with their songs of joy as you do here to-day, will depend largely upon your fidelity to your heaven-appointed trust. You are the keepers of this ancient church; keep it for Christ and the generations yet unborn.

REMARKS OF HON. C. S. SIMS.

Brief Remarks by the Hon. Clifford Stanley Sims of Mount Holly, N. J.

My friends, it would be very difficult, if not impossible, for me to describe to you my emotions as I stand here in the church which was the last charge of my great-great grandfather, the Reverend John Brainerd, and where he lies buried.

There should, however, be no feeling of pride on account of descent from such a man, but rather a feeling of determination to endeavor to always remember his Godly life and to seek to emulate it.

There is but little I can tell you beyond what you already know regarding him. He was born in Haddam, Connecticut, February 28th, 1720; entered Yale College in 1742, and graduated from there in 1746; was licensed as a Minister of the Gospel in 1747; was a Trustee of Princeton College from 1754 until his death; was a Chaplain in the army in 1759, in the Old French War; and was the Moderator of the Old Synod of New York and Philadelphia in 1762; but it is principally as an earnest missionary in this State that we know of him, and the Presbyterian Church in West Jersey owes much to his self-sacrificing labor.

He was an ardent patriot during the Revolutionary War; in 1776 he preached at Blackwoodtown a sermon from Psalm cxliv, 1, "Blessed be the Lord my strength: who teacheth my hands to war and my fingers to fight," and appealed to his congregation to enlist and fight for their country. Finally the British forces burnt his church and house at Mount Holly, and in 1777 he removed here and took charge of this church; and here, March 18th, 1781, he died.

Though a stranger to you all, I venture to urge one thing, namely, that it is almost a duty that some steps should be taken to place in print, and so preserve, a record of the celebration here to-day of an event as remarkable in this country as the one hundred and fiftieth anniversary of the Deerfield Church.

ADDRESS OF REV. ALLEN H. BROWN

On "The Presbyterian Church in South Jersey, its Origin and Progress."

The term South Jersey is here applied to all of New Jersey, south of a line drawn from Sandy Hook through Amboy to Bordentown. Ecclesiastically, it contains the Presbyteries of Monmouth and West Jersey. These two Presbyteries cover nine and a half counties, or more than all the combined territory of the six other Presbyteries of the Synod of New Jersey.*

Among the early settlers of South Jersey were Friends or Quakers, Baptists, and Episcopalians. Some emigrants came from Sweden; Huguenots from France; the Reformed from Holland; Presbyterians came from England, Scotland and Ireland, while from New England and by the way of Long Island, many came to our coast, ascended its rivers where now familiar names of persons and places indicate the origin of the first settlers.

Assembled to celebrate the one hundred and fiftieth anniversary of the organization of the Deerfield Church, let us go back a hundred years or more to learn the condition of the country. In the last century there must have been an intimate relation between the Egg Harbour district, and Pittsgrove and Deerfield.

Enoch Green having been licensed to preach in 1761, labored in Egg Harbour, how long we know not. Thence he was called to settle at Deerfield, and was installed in 1767. He died December 2, 1776.

John Brainerd, failing in health, was called from Egg Harbour missions in 1777, to succeed Mr. Green at Deerfield, but was not installed. Here he died in 1781. Both these men were buried in this church, beneath the aisles, which were originally paved with bricks. Can we recall them from the grave? Enoch Green! John Brainerd! In the spirit world are they cognizant of these scenes? However that may be, they being dead, yet speak to us by their deeds and writings.

---

*Omitting the Presbytery of Corisco in Africa.

In August, 1761, John Brainerd wrote to Mrs. Smith, * "I spend something more than half my Sabbaths here at Brotherton, the rest are divided. At this place I have but few white people. The other places are in the midst of the inhabitants, and whenever I preach there I have a large number of white people that meet to attend divine service. But besides these, I have preached at eight different places on Lord's days, and near twenty on other days of the week, and never fail of a considerable congregation, so large and extensive is this vacancy. Two large counties and a considerable part of two more almost wholly destitute of a preached gospel, except what the Quakers do in their way, and many of the people but one remove from a state of heathenism."

John Brainerd's letter to Enoch Green, earlier in the same year, (June 1861), illustrates both the destitutions of the country and how diligently those men labored to supply the people with the gospel. The field is from Toms River to Tuckahoe. He mentions only one meeting house, but gives the names of seventeen heads of families, at whose houses meetings are usually held, viz: at Toms River, Goodluck, Barnegat, Manahocking, Wading River, Great Egg Harbour and Tuckahoe, and advises Mr. Green to make appointments for Mr. Smith and Mr. McKnight, who will succeed him.

Although Dr. Thomas Brainerd published the life of John Brainerd in a large volume, (492 pages) full justice has not yet been done to his memory.

In 1886 Judge Joel Parker delivered at Mount Holly an address, recounting the work of John Brainerd, and the obligation of the churches of other denominations in that region to his abundant labors. He quotes from a remarkable diary discovered since Dr. Brainerd published the life of John Brainerd. That journal was brought from London by Doctor George Macloskie, when he came to Princeton college. The little book mentioned Princeton, but not the name of the writer. In Princeton, it was proven to be John Brainerd's Journal from January 1761 to October 1762. It is the more valuable because Doctor Brainerd, in his memoir, gives little notice of 1761, and of the year 1762 says, we have no report of Mr. Brainerd's missionary labors this year.

The Diary gives a daily account of incessant itinerant work. Thus Brainerd visited Bridgetown, (now Mount Holly); Bordentown, Wepink, Timber Creek, Woodbury, Salem, Penn's Neck, Cape May, Great Egg Harbour, the Forks of the Little Egg Harbour, Cedar Bridge, Mannahawkin, Toms River, extending over a wide district. He attends to the repair of meeting houses at Timber Creek and Woodbury, promotes a subscription for the support of the Gospel in various places, and at Great Egg Harbour secured a subscription of £80 annually for the support of the Gospel ministry. Well does Doctor Macloskie say, "The Journal furnishes a striking picture of missionary zeal, such as had few parallels in the century to which it belonged."

The Journal of Philip V. Fithian sheds light upon the progress of the Presbyterian Church up to the Revolutionary War. He and Enoch Green married daughters of Beatty. Both were Chaplains in the army. Both died of camp fever. At White Plains Mr. Fithian fought in the ranks. In 1775, or fourteen years after Mr. Green's first missionary tour above mentioned, Mr. Fithian visited a portion of the same district, viz: Egg Harbour and the Forks, and proves that several houses of worship had been erected in the interval. Besides preaching at private houses, Mr. Fithian preached at Mr. Clark's little log meeting house; also at Brotherton and at Clark's Mill meeting house, and at Blackman's meeting house. Other churches are known to have been erected, though not mentioned by Mr. Fithian.

Thus have we noticed the diligent work of itinerants, and the progress of the Presbyterian church up to the Revolutionary War. Then followed times of trial and retrogression, disaster and decline. New Jersey was a battle field. The Presbyterian Church suffered much from the long desolating war, and was impoverished in men and means. None exceeded John Brainerd in zeal for independence. His churches among the Indians disappeared with them. His church at Mount Holly was burned. Rev. Charles McKnight preached at Middletown Point, Shrewsbury and Shark River. He was seized by the British and his church was burned. He died soon after his release in 1778.* Crosswick's church ceased to exist. The site of a church at Middletown is now a tangled thicket. That of Shark River is an open common. The location of Barnegat church, mentioned in Webster's History and in John Griffith's Journal, has not yet been identified. A few grave stones mark the ground which John Leake by his will gave for a Presbyterian meeting house at Wading River in 1777. All the above mentioned were located in the territory of the present Monmouth Presbytery. The churches which survived the war in that portion of South Jersey and came down from the last century were Shrewsbury, which at one time was almost extinct; old Tennent, (or Freehold), Cranbury and Allentown.

In the territory of the present West Jersey Presbytery, we look in vain for Mr. Clark's little log meeting house. A burial ground marks the site of Clark's Mill meeting house; and Blackman's meeting house fell into the possession of the Methodist Church. Long ago the churches of Longacoming, Aloes Creek and Penn's Neck or Quihawken disappeared. The churches which came down to us from the last century now existing in West Jersey Presbytery, are Woodbury, Blackwoodtown, Pittsgrove, Deerfield, Greenwich, Bridgeton, Fairfield, (or Cohansey), and Cape May.

Thus, of our ninety extant churches in South Jersey, only twelve had their origin in the last century. After the Revolutionary war the Old Stone Church was erected at Fairfield, and a brick edifice at Bridgeton was dedicated in 1795. With these exceptions we know of no efforts to build up, much less to extend the Presbyterian Church in West or South Jersey, from the beginning of the war in 1775 to 1820, a period of forty-five years.

In 1820 there was a remarkable revival of missionary zeal, and under the influence of Rev. Jonathan Freeman, of Bridgeton, the Domestic Missionary Society of West Jersey arose and accomplished an important work during the remaining two years of his life.

Then the churches of Salem and Millville were established. The appeals for help from Mr. Freeman and Col. Johnson on behalf of the infant church at Salem might now amuse the good people of that flourishing church. History repeats itself and those appeals should inspire our sympathy and hope for other churches now struggling for existence.

The Presbytery of West Jersey was organized in 1839, and from that time the Presbyterian Church has made steady progress within the six counties which this Presbytery now covers.

In 1840, and for many previous years, in Atlantic county, (or Egg Harbour), we had no church, and now have eight.

In the present Camden County, Blackwoodtown Church then stood alone, now there are nine Presbyterian churches.

In Gloucester County are ten, and all of these excepting Woodbury have been organized since 1840. In Salem County, where were two before 1840, are now four, and in Cape May County, where was one, are also four.

In Cumberland County, always the stronghold of the Presbyterian Church, were eight and now are ten churches.

Thus thirty-five churches have been organized in forty-seven years, and while the population has increased two and one-half times, the membership of our churches has increased about four-fold.

A similar report of progress might be made of Monmouth Presbytery, which was organized first in 1859, and reconstructed in 1870.

History repeats itself and has its lessons:

I. Were the former days better than these? Some assert that our churches in former years did not call for so much financial aid as now, because they sustained the Gospel by uniting contiguous churches, and that therefore we should do the same.

'Tis true that once Woodbury and Pittsgrove were united.

In 1750 the Presbytery of New Brunswick directed as to Penn's Neck and Woodbury, that in the place which provided a house to live in, Mr. Chestnut should preach two-thirds of the time, and in the other one-third. In 1751 the same Presbytery decided that Mr. Hunter should preach at Greenwich one-half, Deerfield one-fourth, and at Pilesgrove one-fourth of his time. In 1794 the two churches, Greenwich and Bridgeton, united in calling Mr. Clarkson. Not until 1823 and 24 did the church of Bridgeton venture to sustain the gospel alone, and then terminated the collegiate relation which had existed for thirty years.

Times have changed, and so have the habits and demands of churches. Do you wish to return to those old times as better than the present? You do not realize the struggles of your Fathers to establish the ordinances which you now enjoy. Place yourselves in their circumstances, if you can, and you will sympathize with other feeble struggling churches of the present day.

II. History teaches us to cultivate diligently the field, which is committed to our care. The churches of Penns Neck and Aloes Creek had vigor enough in 1797 to secure a pastor, and in 1803 had eighty communicants at a time when the two churches of Woodbury and Timber Creek, (Blackwoodtown), were reduced to seven members. Once we wondered what were the causes of the decline of Aloes Creek and Penn's Neck churches. Now we wonder that they lived so long, when we read that for twenty years, and again for nine years, the people had no regular preaching; but only occasional supplies, and for another period of seven years only an annual supply.

Has the Lord committed to us any portion of his vineyard to cultivate for Christ? If we are unfaithful in its cultivation, the Lord of the vineyard will take it away and give it unto other husbandmen.

III. Deerfield owes a debt to Egg Harbour. John Leake waited upon or escorted both Enoch Green and John Brainerd from Egg Harbour to Deerfield. Thus Deerfield church obtained the ministry of the Gospel at the expense of Egg Harbour. Deerfield survived and the churches of Egg Harbour, which were planted by John Brainerd, declined and became extinct.

Suppose the process had been reversed; then Deerfield Church had become extinct. Deerfield owes a debt to Egg Harbour and to John Brainerd, and to the Great Head of the Church.

How shall that debt be repaid?

---

*See the Presbyterian, April 26, 1856.

ADDRESS OF CALEB ALLEN, A. B.

CONDENSED ADDRESS OF MR. ALLEN ON THE "IMPORTANT
EVENTS OF THE PAST ONE HUNDRED AND FIFTY YEARS."

It is my task to outline the progress of events during the
existence of this little church. In the peaceful village of
Deerfield, pastor has succeeded pastor, and generation followed
generation to the "silent city of the dead." Outside this quiet
harbor storms have raged and many a gallant bark has gone to
wreck.

One hundred and fifty years ago! How long—how short
a time! What a trifle of the world's history! But crowded with
events, separated from us by marvellous progress, away in a
past already growing dim—how far distant!

It is impossible to predict the altered circumstances of A.
D. 2037. Almost equally difficult is it to fill in the details of
the distant past. Yet this is just the best way of estimating
the world's progress.

Let us now go back to the "good old times," or if you will
"the bad old times," and first take a peep across the water.
Here comes one of the old-timers. Very stately is he in flowing wig and knee breeches; his long coat adorned with lappels
and side pockets. His house is in keeping with his attire.
In the low ceiled reception room, uncomfortable, straight
backed mahogany chairs stand around the panelled walls in
formal rows, whilst a jingling harpsichord occupies one corner.
In his bed room, a close fusty chamber, hung with dismal dam-
ask, stands the huge fourpost bed, like a gigantic hearse, so
high that steps are needed for the perilous ascent. When he
retires at night he will sleep (if he can) sunk in the center of
a mass of yielding feathers, the bed curtains carefully drawn
and tied to exclude every breath of fresh air; down to his nose
he will draw a thick woolen night cap, and then with the dim
rush light burning in a basin on the floor, he will lie semi-suffo-
cated in what he calls "comfort." His London house stands in
a narrow street, adorned with odoriferous heaps of refuse which

are scattered by the wind for every shower to beat into a thick black paste. A large open drain in close proximity sends pestilential steams into the foul atmosphere. As a man of fashion our friend breakfasts at ten, dines at two, takes tea at five, and sups at eight o'clock. When he gives a dinner he will not fail to send home every guest intoxicated. If a brawl occurs he will arm with pistols and settle his quarrel in a duel. In the intervals of sleeping, eating, drinking and gambling, he will visit the theatre where the coarseness of the scenes will by no means shock his delicacy, or he will watch two men slice each other with broad swords; or at a bull-bait will enjoy the mutual tortures of gored dogs and a chained and infuriated bull. This elegant program will be varied by boxing matches and cock fights. When our friend walks through the city at night he goes cautiously along under the feeble twinkle of the oil lamps, past aged watchmen, who are snoring in their boxes, or trembling lest their old bones should be pounded by the noisy bloods who go reeling by. Happy, indeed, if he is not pounced upon from some dark corner, knocked on the head and robbed.

Such is a fair picture of the life of an English gentleman of 150 years ago. Contrast it with the present; the low, close, stuffy rooms with the well lighted, well ventilated and well warmed modern house; the filthy surroundings with modern sanitary improvements. Think of our healthier habits and more refined pleasures; of profanity and sensuality as no longer characteristic of the gentleman; drinking and gambling under ban; duelling and highway robbery almost things of the past, and you will see the progress of 150 years.

Now let us look at Boston, just after the War for Independence in 1784. From various sources we may learn the condition and customs of the people. Though Boston was the third city in the States, its streets were irregular, the carriage ways were unpaved, and the sidewalks unflagged. The houses were of wood, with unpainted weatherboard sides. Furniture was imported. There were heavy sideboards, English eight-day clocks with chimes, and high candelabra drawn about the floor on rollers. The huge fireplaces were adorned with scripture tiles, and the walls with inartistic colored engravings. In the streets the houses were not numbered, but instead were golden bells, blue gloves, crowns and sceptres, dogs and rainbows, elephants and horse shoes. In the shop of the haberdasher were found wares of strange look and name—lawns and jeans, galloons and silk ferrets, swords, garterings, vest patterns and silk cloaks. The threshing machine, cast iron wheeled plough, drill, potato digger, reaper and binder, hay raker and corn cutter, were all unknown. In the farmer's house paint and carpet, had no existence; beef and pork, salt fish, rye bread, dried apples and vegetables coarsely served made his monotonous fare the year round. His Sunday suit of broadcloth lasted his life and then descended to his son. It is a question which was more to be pitied, the school teacher who itinerated amongst his patrons and gave to their children the elements of education in return for his board; or the unfortunate school boy, to whom hard fare, sermons, prayers and floggings came round with distressing regularity. The village doctor pounded his own drugs, prepared his own medicines, and put up his own prescriptions. He bled and cupped and leached unmercifully; of quinine, ether and chloroform, he was profoundly ignorant, and vaccination was as yet undreamed of. Even in the northern cities the dead cart nightly shot the victims of yellow fever into the pits of the Potter's field. But highest in dignity stood the minister. To sit patiently on the rough board seats while he turned the hourglass for the third time, was a delectable privilege. His sermon was the great event of the week. The newspapers were wretched productions on miserable paper, and never appeared oftener than three times a week. News was conspicuous by its absence. Travelling was perilous. Before a journey men made their wills and said to their friends a sad farewell. Two stages carried all the passengers between New York and Boston. The travelers had often to help drag the clumsy vehicle out of the slough. The condition of the poor was most wretched. Only by the strictest economy could the mechanic keep out of jail. His home was comfortless. Stoves, coal and matches were things unheard of. Worst of all, if misfortune overtook him he was liable to be seized by the Sheriff and hurried to prison for debt. And the prisons were horrible. To loss of liberty and the bitter thought of starving children at home, were added the terrors of the treadmill, the pillory, the stocks, the shears, the branding iron and the lash.

Vast has been the progress since that day. Manners have changed, and morals. The spirit of humanity, has grown. Mechanical inventions and discoveries have increased the happiness of our race. From feebleness and poverty the country has progressed to power and wealth. Education, a free press, a free church, the influence and power of religion have produced and are still producing their marvellous transformation.

For the great and stirring events which have begotten nations and remodelled maps; for the startling discoveries which have given to mankind new creations for good, and terrific forces for evil; for the enterprise that has set on foot vast undertakings, and opened up unknown worlds; for the new ideas which so powerfully are influencing men's minds for weal or woe, but little space is left. Nor is much required. To us they are familiar as our daily bread.

Europe has been remodeled. Asia and Africa are opened up. South America is independent. Thirteen states have developed to thirty-eight. The Civil War has been fought. Slavery has been abolished and the united nation is daily growing stronger for its part in the world's destiny.

Christianity has modified the horrors of war, and the Red Cross, the emblem of peace, is borne into the midst of its carnage. The revolver, the repeating breech loader, the torpedo boat, the ironclad, the monstrous 100-ton gun;—all doubtful triumphs, yet it may be hastening the universal peace.

The steamboat and locomotive, the safety lamp, coal gas, natural gas, electricity, vaccination, the great iron and cotton industries, iron puddling, the spinning jenny, the water frame, the mule, and the power loom, Congreve rockets, percussion locks, the kaleidoscope, lucifer matches, sewing machines, telegraphs and telephones, steam hammers, gun cotton and dynamite, light houses and life boats, the penny post, photography, Atlantic cables, submarine tunnels, Alpine railways, diving bells and dresses, sanitary reform and police; these are the children of the last 150 years of history. These have caused 1737 to be as far behind us, as Julius Caesar is behind it.

And the great world has opened up Africa. Australia, Central Asia, China, Japan, Corea, New Guinea, and the islands of the South Seas, mostly unknown to 1737, are yielding to the power of the Cross. The march has been ever forward. Receding here, advancing there, our holy religion like a mighty tide has swept on in its irresistible course, and in no distant future shall cover the whole earth, "for the mouth of the Lord hath spoken it."

The Committee failed to secure the address of Rev. Robert J. Burtt, of Marksboro, N. J. Repeated attempts were made to obtain it for publication, but without success. It is to be regretted that this link of the chain of proceedings must be left out.

ADDRESS OF MR. C. S. TYLER.

Like our friend, who, as the representative of the sainted John Brainerd, addressed us this morning, I came to-day to remain one of the unknown among this great gathering, but during the recess at noon I went down to the old historic spring to drink where my fathers drank; I cannot say that I drank in any inspiration. When coming away I met a friend, whose native modesty would not permit him to mention the subject himself, concerning the propriety of having the fact stated upon a stone beside the church, setting forth the many virtues of Rev. Enoch Green; that his body is not beneath the stone, but resting still within these walls. With this in view and to also enquire about the stone covering the grave of John Brainerd, which years ago I saw along the aisle before me, but which to-day, seeking it, I failed to find. Whilst looking for some of the "heads of this meeting" to confer about those matters, I fell into the hands of your pastor, and the expectations of the morning came to an end.

As I wandered among those numerous and nameless graves, I could but wonder where among them repose the ashes of my ancestors? As I look over this great assembly, I see many descendants of those who, taking their lives in their hands, defied the wrath of Pope, Priests, and King at Boyne Water and Derry. Although they were men of humble lives, unknown to history and fame, I am prouder of a descent from such an ancestry, than I should be for the right to "the quartering" upon the shield of the Queen of England, or that of any other royal family.

We are told that certain traits of character are transmitted from parents to children; may it not be that the same spirit that worked in the fathers beyond the sea, to there establish civil and religious liberty, moved also, though in a less notable manner, in the hearts and lives of the founders of this church? May it not have been something of that same spirit of endurance that led the mothers of a century ago, whenever the weather permitted—to gather such of their children as were able for such a journey, and walk to church from Deerfield to Greenwich; walking those weary miles of roads, not laid out as we now know them, but winding through most open places of the heavy timber lands of that day, and by their many turns adding much to the distance; and often were they in the condition of those described by the gentleman that preceded me—walking in heat as hard to bear as any that we have experienced in the weeks just past; days we found so hot and exhausting that many thought they could not possibly go up to His house to hear the word of the Lord.

Is it any wonder that out from under such training there went forth men willing to endure all the hardships and perils of our Revolutionary struggles, and those earlier colonial wars that were not alone contests for life and home, but for Protestantism as well.

My heart has been stirred by the events of to-day, and thoughts of the past have flown as with wings. Here in your midst I was born; here in this house I was consecrated to God; here among these seats, from this pulpit, I first heard the way of life—though true, there is now no memory of those words. And now after this lapse of time, I am glad to-day to assure you that during all the years following the period when ill health severed the connection between pastor and people, there remained, and does still remain, with surviving head of *that* parsonage household, a strong feeling of friendship for the people that were left behind; with hearty good wishes for those that from time to time had given the hand, and spoken the words of cheer to the pastor and his young wife.

To-day we have listened to many evidences of kind feeling on the part of the people of this church for their several pastors. To-day we look abroad over your hills, and fertile fields, where roam your many herds, or are glorious in promise of the coming harvest; and the thought has come, may it not be that this increase in basket and in store, that has brought joy to your lives, has come in answer to the prayers of God's servants? heaven's reward for favors to them; favors that could not be returned in kind.

This morning as we listened to those recollections that stirred our hearts, we were asked, "What shall be the record of the church at the end of the second century, when its history shall be read?" What the record of the next fifty years shall be, will depend entirely upon yourselves; what you shall do and train your children to do, for the advancement of God's kingdom and cause. If you gain no inspiration from the lives and efforts of those that have gone before you, who wrought that you might to-day rejoice; if from the things of to-day there comes no incentive to greater exertion for the years to come; if you and your children shall sit down content only to rejoice in the accomplishments of the past hundred and fifty years, then for those that shall gather here in 1937, there can be nothing but disappointment and regret in view of the failures of those fifty years.

God seems to have wonderfully favored you at this time in granting so perfect a day, that none should be hindered in coming to this place to rejoice and praise Him for His wonderful work of the past. I think this beautiful day, with all its favorable circumstances, has been granted not alone that you might gather to rejoice over what our fathers accomplished, but that nothing should hinder a gathering for instruction and warnings as well. We have just listened to the history of the rise, progress, and in some cases the decay and death, of Presbyterian churches in South Jersey: an encouragement to us as we have seen how, through adversity, and many and long struggles, some churches have grown strong and flourishing, and a warning, as we have listened to the story of the decline and death of others. And I have in mind one, that in generations ago was supplanted by another denomination, (Logtown or Harmersville). Whether they died as a church through "a famine of hearing the word," or because they failed as Presbyterians to do what they should, and might have done for the country around them I know not; yet this is known, that those who took their place, and have held that region of country as one of the strongholds of that denomination, have not done through the succeeding years what they should, and might have done, for those within their bounds. To-day, another denomination has entered upon the field, and whether they in turn shall possess it, will in a great measure depend upon the way in which the former shall use their opportunities in advancing God's kingdom, and benefitting their fellow men.

And now the day hastens to its close, and these anniversary exercises will be a matter of the past, and the history of another half century will commence, to end with a record depending entirely upon what you as a church shall do. Shall it be the record of a people who drew lessons of encouragement and warning from their history of the past, an inspiration, an incentive to greater zeal for the years to come, who increased their efforts to meet the great and growing needs of year by year, not only around them at home, but abroad throughout the land? a work to be done, an obligation resting upon you, not alone as Presbyterians, but as christians and patriots as well.

May God grant that from this day's gathering there shall go forth an influence that shall make you flourishing, and strong for all that pertains to God's kingdom and glory.

ADDRESS OF REV. J. D. HUNTER.

CONDENSED ADDRESS OF MR. HUNTER ON "THE SABBATH
SCHOOL, ITS HISTORY AND WORK."

In the brilliant procession of important events during the last one hundred and fifty years, none attract the attention of earnest, thoughtful men, more than the three most significant moral monuments since the days of the Apostles, except perhaps, the reformation movement of the sixteenth century. I mean the Missionary, the Temperance, and the Sunday School movements. All three of these movements, now absorbing so much of the thought and effort of the Christian Church, have been inaugurated within the lifetime of the Deerfield Church. There were missionaries, of course, before Carey and Mills, but no systematic plans for the evangelization of the world. There were Temperance reformers before Benjamin Rush, but no determined effort based upon scientific truth. There were Sunday Schools before Robert Raikes, but no well defined system whereby their permanent establishment and universal extension might be secured.

It is just as difficult to trace the Sunday School idea to its origin as it is to do so of any other great thought. Before a new idea is born into the world, the spirit of truth seems to brood over the earth, finally depositing its precious offspring wherever there is an open, progressive, willing mind. In speaking of original ideas, then, we must understand that an idea may originate with a great many different persons.

Then, further, we must distinguish between a thought involved in a principle, and the same thought incorporated in an institution. There is always a principle back of every institution, older than the institution. Back of the idea of the Raikes Sunday School is the older idea of the principal underlying the Raikes Sunday School. The principle upon which the Raikes Sunday School was founded is more than four thousand years old. I mean the principle that it is the duty of the church to care for and religiously train the young. Dr. H.

Clay Trumbull, in his excellent work, "Teachers and Teaching," clearly traces and distinguishes this principle back in the days of Abraham. He correctly distinguishes three agencies in the church for the religious training of the race—the Family, the Church-school, and the Pulpit. For fifteen hundred years the Family was the sole agency. During this time it demonstrated its inability alone to properly train the race. So God ordained the Church-school, not to displace the Family, but to co-operate with it. The Pulpit was first permanently established in the days of John the Baptist. Prior to that the mission of the preacher or prophet was only occasional. This Church School involved the principle underlying the modern Sunday School.

There was the germ at least of a Sunday School at Taunton, England, in 1638; at Ephrata, Lancaster Co., Pa., in 1744; at Catterick, England, in 1763; and in numerous other places in obscure localities in England, Scotland, and America. But the Raikes school was distinct from all these previous efforts in the following particulars: (1) They were confined to the children of the church, while Raikes' idea was to include all; (2) they were taught in one class and by the pastor, while the Raikes school was divided into classes and taught by laymen; (3) they studied only the catechisms of the churches, while in the Raikes schools they also taught reading and spelling, and memorized scripture; (4) they were denominational and local, while the Raikes schools were unsectarian and for universal extension; (5) they were not known by any name that has come down to us, while the Raikes schools are the first to bear the name of Sunday School.

It is sometimes questioned whether what are known as the Raikes schools were really originated by him. Some would have it that Rev. Thomas Stock, contemporary and friend of Raikes, is the real "father of the Sunday school." The facts seem to be then concerning the starting of the first distinctive Raikes Sunday School: (1) Raikes accidentally learns of the ignorance and viciousness of great numbers of the poor children of his native town of Gloucester; (2) he is set to thinking of some way to better the condition of the neglected children, and recalls something that had been tried by a Mr. King, a wealthy manufacturer of a neighboring town, in the way of gathering the children into a school on Sundays; (3) he resolves to try something of the same sort in Gloucester, and immediately employs four lady teachers to take charge of as many children as he should send, promising to pay these teachers a shilling a day for their labor; (4) Raikes then calls upon Rev. Thomas Stock to make known his plans and to seek his assistance; (5) Stock had been thinking of something of the same sort, and falls right in with Raikes, and together they go out to hunt up scholars to begin with, and succeed in finding ninety willing to enroll. And thus it is that the first real Sunday School was organized and started, in Gloucester, July 1780.

Who is this Robert Raikes, upon whom such great honor has come? Was he some religious fanatic or wild enthusiast? What sort of a brain conceived the idea of the modern Sunday School? It was just two years before your fathers organized this Church here at Deerfield that Robert Raikes first saw the light over there in England, in the town of Gloucester. His father was a successful journalist; his mother was the daughter of Rev. Richard Drew. Robert entered the profession of his father, and at the early age of twenty-two became the sole proprietor and editor of his father's paper, the "Gloucester Journal." This paper he edited with distinguished ability. His editorials were extensively copied, even the metropolitan journals of London quoting liberally from them. He had a large brain, a profound understanding, a great mastery of language, and a forceful style. He advocated many reforms, and especially reform in the management of prisons. Socially he was received into the highest ranks, being on intimate terms with royalty. Were I to seek some one here at home to liken him to, I could do no better perhaps than to compare him to the late Horace Greeley or to the journalist and philanthropist of Philadelphia, George W. Childs.

Four years after the first school was organized a dozen more had sprung up in that same county of Gloucestershire, and one had been organized in the metropolis of London by the congregation of the celebrated Rowland Hill, of Surry Chapel. In one short decade England alone has over a thousand schools, with sixty-four thousand scholars. At Windsor, ladies of fashion passed their Sundays in teaching the poorest children. Mrs. Sarah Trimmer, popular authoress and magazine editor, was an active worker in these first Sunday Schools. And Hannah More, the gifted writer of prose poetry of the last century, organized a flourishing school of her own.

But England has never entirely gotten away from the narrow notion of the first promoters of Sunday Schools; the notion that only children of the ignorant and poorer classes stand in need of Sunday Schools. The children of the "respectable" people, of the high-born and high-standing, even when church people, are not in the schools. The children of church officers, ministers and deacons, as a rule, are not in the English Sunday Schools. All this is very primitive.

The first Sunday School, proper, in the United States, was organized in Hanover county, Va., in 1786, by Francis Asbury, the patriarch of American Methodism. To-day they number 99,762 schools, 1,107,170 teachers, and 8,034,478 scholars, making a grand total of over 9,000,000! But there is almost an equal army of youth, under school age, not enrolled in any Sunday School, here in our own land!

Scotland—Presbyterian Scotland—at first determined to have nothing to do with Sunday Schools. Where was the layman's Divine right to teach? And dare anyone profane the Sabbath by engaging in Sunday School work on that day? So the good orthodox Scotch preacher, who loved his toddy, and took such delight in cock-fights, threatened to ex-communicate any parent who should send his children to these unauthorized, unholy Sunday Schools. Sunday School teachers were really arrested and brought into Aberdeen, under escort of constables, as the veriest criminals of the land. This was when schools first began to be organized, say in 1788 or 1790. In time things changed, prejudice ceased. But the Scotch have never been a very enthusiastic Sunday School people.

Free thinking and Roman Catholic France is coming under the power of the Sunday School. In Italy and in Spain many Protestant Sunday Schools are composed almost entirely of Roman Catholic children. May it not be that the Sunday School is destined to become the dynamite to blow into atoms the Roman Vatican?

Rationalistic Germany has 300,000 children in the Sunday Schools; and although the secular press is quite generally hostile, there is no country in Europe where the Sunday School cause is so prosperous to-day.

In little more than a century the seeming insignificant school of ninety scholars on the British Isle, has grown to be a host of 16,447,990 scholars, reaching the world over!

This wonderful success has been possible only by associated effort. So early as 1785 a "Union" was formed in London to extend Sunday Schools in the British dominions. In 1795 Scotland had a similar association for that country. In 1824 the "American Sunday School Union" was organized. The most efficient of these associations is the "Foreign Sunday School Association." In our own country the different states for the most part have their unions or associations. Eight states have every county organized, three of which have every township—Connecticut, Maryland and New Jersey.

The "International Sunday School Convention" meets triennially. The first met in 1875, in Baltimore. Since then the Convention has been held at Atlanta, Toronto, Louisville, and Chicago. This "International" was the outgrowth of a "National Convention" which met first in 1832.

It was at the last "National Convention," at Indianapolis, in 1872, that the "International Lesson System" was adopted. For some years previously there had been uniform lessons adopted in certain localities, but now it was first proposed to make uniform lessons extend to all schools throughout the world. An "International Lesson Committee," consisting of fourteen members, was appointed for a term of seven years. At the end of that time a similar committee was to be appointed by the "International Convention." Each committee selects the lessons for seven years, going through the Bible in course.

This system has been severely criticised. It has been called the "game of hop, skip and jump." The objection is not to the uniform feature, except so far as it applies to all grades of scholars. The point criticised most severely is the changing about of the lessons from one part of the Bible to another. The question stood thus: Shall we have graded lessons for different ages and different conditions, or shall we have graded helps and teaching with uniform lessons? Thus stated all can see how uniform lessons may be made suitable to all ages and conditions. The greatest weakness of the system is the flitting about feature. This may and ought to be remedied.

The proper organization of the individual school demands the most intelligent consideration. Most schools now are "church" schools, rather than "union" or "undenominational." The pastor is the head of the school ex-officio. The church directly, or through her spiritual advisers, should have an influential part in selecting the officers and teachers. The qualification of the teacher actually to train the scholar should receive more attention. There are too many youthful teachers in our schools. A high grade of teaching is necessary in order to win and retain the patronage of intelligent parents.

We must do more work and better, if we would save the American boys and girls. Remember, if we save the boys and girls of the present, we save the men and women of the future. As Wordsworth says, "The boy is farther to the man." What are boys good for? queried a Sunday School orator. "To make men of," replied a little urchin who spoke more wisely than he knew. Our times sorely need honest, pure, sober, law-abiding men. Look at our daily papers! They are scarcely more than catalogues of daily crimes! Some vigorous Sunday School teaching has got to be done. We must instill the decalogue into the hearts of the youth; nor must we be content with mere morality. Pope was mistaken when he wrote, "An honest man is the noblest work of God." Young stated a profounder truth when he said, "The Christian is the highest style of man." The Christian type of manhood should be the goal towards which every Sunday School teacher should be working.

REV. DAVID M. JAMES' ADDRESS.

With feelings mingled in joy and sadness, I return after an absence of many years, to take part in this hundred and fiftieth anniversary. I rejoice at this outlook. The enlargement and beautifying of this house; the improved increase of the congregation; the advancement and favorable improvement of all the surroundings.

When I left this place in the days of my youth, I was acquainted with almost every person who worshipped here. I could call every name. Now as I glance over this large assembly I can hardly recognize a countenance. The faces and forms of those who were then so familiar have departed. We do not see them on the streets, nor in the homes they then occupied, but we read their names on the stones and monuments which symbolize the affection of surviving friends, and the faith that they have entered into rest.

But the church and the ordinances of God remain, confirming the truth of His Word, "That one generation passeth away, and another cometh, but the earth abideth forever."

I wish to bear testimony to the value of good religious training here in early life. The prayers of a pious mother, the preaching of the gospel by the pastors, the instructions in the Sabbath School by kind and devoted teachers, the reading of good books, and the prayers of the aged Elders—all assisted in making a foundation for my Christian life.

Then I have a vivid impression of the school teachers—of David Shute and Mark Peck, who used to flog the boys for doing nothing, telling them, at the same time, that this was the reason why, because we were sent to school to do something.

I am reminded of an incident of an English land-holder, who was requested by one of his tenants to assign to him an acre of land on which he might have the privilege of raising one crop. The request was so singular and earnest, that the landlord granted the tenant his petition. The tenant prepared the land and sowed his seed, but it was many months before the land holder could understand what the crop would be.   A year passed by, and when the seed sprang up he learned to his surprise that the tenant had sowed acorns. He hadpromised the land for *one crop*, and he must give it time.   Long after the owner of the land and the sower of the seed had passed away, the oaks remained and grew, casting their strong roots into the ground and spreading out their long branches to the breeze.

In like manner we are tenants of Christ, who is the great land-holder. We are sowers of the seed. The good seed is the Gospel of the Kingdom. *We can raise but one crop.* The field is the world. The soil is the heart of every child; sow the good seed on that acre. "Whatsoere a man soweth that shall he also reap."

The sowers who cast in the seed years ago have entered into their rest, but the seed still grows. And herein is that saying true, "One soweth and another reapeth, and gathereth fruit unto eternal life, that both he that soweth and he that reapeth may rejoice together."

ADDRESS OF REV. WM. H. JAMES, D. D.

SUBSTANCE OF THE REMARKS MADE BY REV. WM. H. JAMES, D. D., ONE OF THE SONS OF THE CHURCH.

It has been my privilege during my long absence from this place, to visit many localities, and to enter many churches in my attendance upon Presbyteries, Synods and General Assemblies, but I enter this church with feelings different from those which I have in worshiping in any other place. Here is my birth-right. This is my inheritance. Here I was dedicated to God in baptism. This is the first house of worship I ever entered. It is the first one I can remember. Here I was instructed in the principles of our holy religion, and taught lessons of divine truth in the Sabbath School. My mind goes back this evening to those days of childhood. I picture before me the church with its four pillars, before it was enlarged, and the people as they sat each in their place in the house of God for worship. Their names and faces are familiar to me. I also remember where they lived in the community. A few remain to this present, but most of them are fallen asleep. I will name some of them: A. M. Woodruff, David Padgett, Aaron Padgett, Dr. J. W. Ludlam, Lucius Moore, Joel Moore, Charles Garrison, David O. Garrison, Jeremiah Parvin, Henry Ott, Ephraim Cory, Elijah Riley, Daniel T. J. Davis, John More, Robert More, Lewis Garrison, Azariah More, Samuel Barker, James J. Davis, Arthur Davis, Enos Davis, Shepherd West, Enoch Paulin, Abijah Shull, William Parvin, Ephraim B. Davis, Daniel Dare, William Conklin, Lewis Moore, John Garrison, Jeremiah Hitchner, Samuel Leake, George W. More, Martin Ott, James More, David Veal, William Null, Alfred Davis, Ephraim Davis, James Davis, Abijah Hand, David Cake, David Findley, Isaac Whitaker, David Paris, Archibald Shimp, Enoch Shoemaker, and a number of others whose names do not at this moment occur to me. I remember their families, their wives and children, as they were seated together in the sanctuary. I also well remember a certain pew where on the Lord's day could be found, with great regularity, a devout worshiper, with her children, seated by her side. It was my honor to call that person mother. To her I owe more than to any other what I am, and what by divine grace I hope to be. She was the most priceless earthly gift that God has ever bestowed upon me. Emotions of deepest gratitude fill my heart this night, that I ever had such a mother. She consecrated me to God and to his service. I can never remember the time, even in my earliest childhood, when I did not desire to be a minister. It was as a fire shut up in my bones. God in his own time and way brought me into his services and into the ministry of his Son.

During the exercises of this day there has been much said about the ministers and ruling elders of this church. This is all well; they have been a power for good here; they have served their generation according to the will of God. But I apprehend that the greatest spiritual power this church has had, has been the godly women who have been in it. No doubt many other sons of this church could testify to the rich spiritual blessings they have enjoyed through a pious parentage. It is fitting that we, their children, should rise up and on this anniversary day call them blessed. As the work and service of the mothers in Israel has not been brought into special prominence in the remarks that have preceded, I take great pleasure in bringing into grateful remembrance their love and devotion to this house of the Lord. And I have a strong impression, from all my experience as a pastor, that the women of this church, at the present time, are an indispensable part of its strength and efficiency.

As one coming home from a long absence and beholding what I see to-day, I am impressed with the fact that while the fathers and mothers pass away, the church still lives. It is a place where "lively stones," "polished after the similitude of a palace," are prepared for the building of God, the house not made with hands, eternal in the heavens.

Who is there who is not ready to join in the prayer, "O God of hosts look down from Heaven, and behold and visit this vine; and the vineyard which thy right hand hath planted, and the branch that thou madest strong for thyself."

ADDRESS OF REV. F. R. BRACE

CONDENSED ADDRESS BY MR. BRACE ON "THE CHURCH AND WHY WE SHOULD LOVE IT."

Coming together as we do, in a place made sacred by hallowed associations, connected with the past one hundred and fifty years, it seems very right and proper that we should turn our thoughts for a little while to that which has given to this place its sacred character. It is not this material edifice that has stood the storms of one hundred and sixteen years, that is older even than the nation whose starry banner is now the emblem of its protection, that gives the sacred character to the place; nor is it the ancient burying ground which surrounds this building, in which lies the precious dust of the beloved ones who have been taken out of the homes, and from the loving embrace of those who would willingly have given their lives for them—the precious dust of the honored servants of God, who have proclaimed the love of God from the pulpit. I know that very loving thoughts wrap themselves around this building. It is a wonderful memorial of great things that have been wrought in many souls during all these past years. It is a reminder of precious gatherings of God's people, of the sweet worship of God, of the union in worship of beloved families, some of whose members are now worshiping in the temple above. And I know that very tender and precious thoughts must go out continually to the quiet home for the dead, that surrounds this building, where lie the remains of those who have fallen asleep, fathers, mothers, husbands, wives, and tender little nurslings.

That, however, which gives sacredness to this place is this: This building is the material inclosure in which the servants of God have met and engaged in the worship of God; it is the temple in which has been enshrined the invisible Christ; the mountain of God from whence has gone forth both the law and the gospel; the house of God where His people have come to meet Him, the gathering place for His church.

And what is the church? It is impossible to unfold all that is expressed in this royal word. We can learn somewhat of its meaning by turning to the sacred scriptures. It is the *ecclesia* of God, the great company that have been called out from the world to become the servants of the living God, those who have heard the voice of God, calling them from sin, from worldliness to a Saviour, to eternal life; the great assemblage of men and women who have in penitence bowed down before the cross of Jesus Christ, confessed their sins and accepted salvation from Him; the company of the blood-bought, blood-washed disciples of the adorable Redeemer; those upon whose brows is written the name of our God and the name of the city of our God.

It is the Kingdom of the Saviour, where he rules and reigns, where his word is law and his wish the motor of every heart, where he sways a sceptre of glory and benignity, and confers on every subject the glory of his own royalty—a kingdom of justice, but when the justice has been maintained and satisfied by the king himself, a kingdom of love where every service is performed, and every duty done out of this highest and holiest, and sweetest motive of love, where not to perform duty, not to engage in service, would be more wearisome, more distasteful, than the hardest service or the most onerous duty—a kingdom where every subject stands and shall stand, as one of the royal family, kings unto God for ever and ever.

It is the flock of the Lord Jesus Christ, carefully and kindly watched over by the Good Shepherd, led into green pastures and beside still waters, the lambs tenderly taken up in His great loving arms or carried in His bosom, the aged ones led carefully and surely along easy pathways. It is the household and family of God, composed of the children of God, those who by His grace have been called from the world and from sin, to take a place in His family and in His house. It is here where the riches of the great fatherly heart of God, of the tenderly loving heart of the Saviour, are constantly made known. Within the walls of this loving home are found all things that can be provided by the Father to make it the best place for His children. Everything needed for nourishment, for comfort, for happiness is provided; bread of life, and fruit of life, for every one that hungers; water of life for every one that thirsts; arbors of refreshment for all that are weary; scenes of beauty and songs of joy for every heart. A blessed household and family is the church of God. Blessed are those who have been adopted into the family of God, who have been enabled to look upward and with uplifted hands and bounding hearts say, Abba Father.

It is the bride of Christ. Never did heart of manliest man go out in strong true currents of pure love towards the woman, who has become to him the highest and loftiest ideal of sweet pure womanhood, as the love of Jesus Christ goes out to His Bride, the Church. All that affection can lavish, or love conceive, or imagination devise, has been wrapped around this bride of Christ. He clothes her Himself in richest and most royal apparel; her clothing is of wrought gold. He bestows upon her not merely the half of His Kingdom, but out of the great love He has to her, He opens all the infinite treasure of His vast Kingdom to her and places them at her disposal. For her, He let His heart's blood flow freely. It was no sacrifice to Him, so great was His love toward her. Yea, He went through the darkest, the most tempestuous night the world ever saw. He fought the fiercest battle that ever mortal or angel witnessed. He endured the agony of crucifixion and the thorns of death for her, and then triumphant over all, was a mighty conqueror, so that He might have her for His own through all the ages to beautify her as He pleases, to enrich her according to the munificence of His own nature, to glorify her before the ranks of the great hierarchies of the heavenly world, and to show through her to the principalities and powers of the world of glory the vast reaches of His own infinite wisdom.

Glorious is the church of God around which the thoughts of God have been wrapped during all the ages, out to which the richest desires of the heart of Christ have been flowing continually, and for which he died, making His blood the purchase price of its future, everlasting happiness.

Let me speak to you of its precious ordinances. How sweet they are to the soul! How many burdens have been rolled off poor, weary hearts, as they have bowed in prayer with the congregation of God's people? How close the Saviour has come to hearts that have been thirsting for Him? How many songs of the sanctuary have been made swift chariots of God to carry the worshipers up to the Upper Sanctuary? Pisgah's top has been reached and the sweet fields, clothed in living green, have been surveyed; Tabor has had its multitudes with the favored three on its summit to look out upon the splendor of the transfigured Lord; earth has been lifted to heaven and the earthly sanctuary transformed to the heavenly. Not only has there been a mingling with the hosts of the heavenly world, but a blending of voices in the great hallelujahs; not only has the outer circle of the worshipers been reached, but even the very foot of the Eternal Throne.

What messages of love have been delivered from its pulpits by the ambassadors of Christ! What tender pleadings with men and women to listen to the offer of Christ and accept His salvation! And sometimes what fearful portrayals of impending wrath and judgment to warn sinners to flee from the wrath to come! What scenes of devout dedication of little children in baptism have been witnessed! What scenes of consecration of mature men and women! But more sweetly solemn than all have been the gatherings of the followers of the Saviour around His table, on which have been spread the emblems of His dying love, when Calvary has once more come before them with its cross and its crucified one. They see the pierced hands and the pierced feet, and the anguished brow. They ask:

"Was it for crimes that I had done,
He groaned upon the tree,
Amazing pity, grace unknown,
And love beyond degree."

And so we love the church, because it is so dear to God, because it is so dear to Christ, because it is worth so much to us. We love it, because it is the channel through which ordinarily the grace of God is brought to man; because through it the great truths of God's love and God's salvation are made known; because it is constantly opening wide its doors of entrance to men and women who long for better things than earth can give, for sweeter joys, wider fellowship, holier communion; because under the wonderful, love-inspiring power of its Head, it stretches its arms of invitation to those who are weary and worn and forlorn and sinful and lost. We love the church because we have so often found God there, when our hearts have been thirsting for Him as in a dry and thirsty land, where no water is; when we have been longing to see His power and glory as they have been seen in the sanctuary; because we have had shed upon us then the mighty power of the Spirit of God, as we have bowed ourselves at the blood-sprinkled mercy seat.

We love it, because of the help and the strength, and the joy it has brought to so many of those whom we have loved, whom we still love, who have done with the cares and the toils of earth. We love it because it contains the great host of the followers of the Redeemer, who have been washed and cleansed in His precious blood. We love it, because the song of joy begun here is to deepen into the great hallelujah yonder, because the stream of peace begun here is to increase into an infinite ocean yonder; because the tiny gleams of love we get here are to spread into the glorious radiance of the full noon-day yonder. We can all say:

"Beyond my highest joy, I prize her heavenly ways,
Her sweet communion, solemn vows, Her hymns of love
    and praise.
Sure as thy truth shall last, To Zion shall be given
The brightest glories earth can yield, And brighter bliss
    of heaven."